Françoise Sagan

Twayne's World Authors Series

French Literature

David O'Connell, Editor

University of Illinois, Chicago

TWAS 797

FRANÇOISE SAGAN
(b. 1935)
Photograph courtesy of Editions Gallimard: Jacques Robert, N.R.F.

Françoise Sagan

By Judith Graves Miller

University of Wisconsin-Madison

Twayne Publishers
A Division of G. K. Hall & Co. • *Boston*

Françoise Sagan
Judith Graves Miller

Copyright 1988 by G. K. Hall & Co.
All rights reserved.
Published by Twayne Publishers
A Division of G. K. Hall & Co.
70 Lincoln Street
Boston, Massachusetts 02111

Copyediting supervised by Barbara Sutton
Book production by Gabrielle B. McDonald
Book design by Barbara Anderson

Typeset in 11 pt. Garamond
by Compset, Inc., of Beverly, Massachusetts

Printed on permanent/durable acid-free paper
and bound in the United States of America

Library of Congress Cataloging-in-Publication Data

Miller, Judith Graves.
    Françoise Sagan / by Judith Graves Miller.
        p.   cm.—(Twayne's world authors series ; TWAS 797. French
    literature)
    Bibliography: p.
    Includes index.
    ISBN 0-8057-8228-1 (alk. paper)
    1. Sagan, Françoise, 1935–   —Criticism and interpretation.
I. Title.   II. Series: Twayne's world authors series ; TWAS 797.
III. Series: Twayne's world authors series. French literature.
PQ2633.U74Z76   1988   87-33114
843'.914—dc19   CIP

To my mother who has never stopped making things possible for me; to David, Kate, Anne, and Judy who keep me believing that the possible is worth the trouble; and to the memory of Jacques Poulet who would not entertain the possible as a solution.

Contents

About the Author

Judith Graves Miller has been teaching French language and literature since 1975. She is currently professor of French at the University of Wisconsin–Madison where her activities include staging annually a full-length play in French with her students. Her productions have ranged from her own adaptations of Flaubert's *Bouvard et Pécuchet* and of Perrault's fairy tales and Diop's African tales, to the Théâtre du Soleil's *1789 ou La Révolution doit s'arrêter à la perfection du bonheur* and Apollinaire's *Les Mamelles de Tirésias*. Dr. Miller is the author of *French Theatre and Revolution Since 1968* (French Forum Monographs, 1977) and numerous studies and review articles on contemporary French theater, treating, among others, the works of Aimé Césaire, Marguerite Duras, Hélène Cixous, Peter Brook, the Théâtre de la Salamandre, and Samuel Beckett. With Professor Christiane Makward of Penn State University, she is now completing translations and introductions for an anthology of ten plays by French and Francophone women writers.

Preface

To label Françoise Sagan a "popular writer" means that one understands the epithet according to its several possible connotations. First though not foremost is a loyal readership that prompts French bookstores, even in staid cities like Metz, to announce her latest work by emptying their windows and displaying a simple sign: "The new Sagan has arrived."[1] Like each autumnal yield of Beaujolais Nouveau (advertised in similar fashion), Sagan's novels, plays, and collections of short stories—twenty-five works since the controversial 1954 triumph of *Bonjour Tristesse*—have their connoisseurs. And like Beaujolais, some vintages prove more polished, more pithy, and more mood-enhancing than others. No matter. The faithful have assured that Sagan has never produced less than a best-seller.

But Françoise Sagan is not only "popular" because her books sell. Her novels also fit into the category of "popular literature": she writes easily readable and mostly enviably honed romances, whose good bad girls, moneyed classes, and glamorous Parisian life-styles recall certain of the fantasy elements of *Dallas* or *Dynasty*. Her romances provide vehicles for mythological topoi—for example, the quest for paradise on earth through unabashed sexuality and total independence, or the celebration of freedom afforded by fast cars and the advent of technology—that have influenced not just French culture but also all of Western "mythology" since the end of World War II. These myths may even reflect in part the effect of American popular culture on European mind-sets.

Sagan's theater likewise takes on a fantastical cast, powering through whimsical plots imaginative flights from middle-class conformity. Moreover, each theatrical production, graced by the collaboration of *haute-couturiers* and movie stars and recorded obsessively by the paparazzi who have followed Sagan throughout her career, becomes in its own right mythic. A Saganian theater event is grist for the mill of the popular imagination.

Sagan herself has attained the status of popular legend. Commentator Bertrand Poirot-Delpech delights in comparing her to "a bird fallen from the nest on which modern cannibalism [meaning the fraternity of reporters, gossip columnists, and their readers] cut its teeth and won't give up."[2] Yet Sagan has, of her own accord, encouraged this attention in myriad interviews and in her autobiographical writings by detailing piquant adventures and suggesting correspondences between herself and her heroines.

In this study I will examine these various aspects of Sagan's popularity. I will analyze especially the pleasure her fantasies give, taking as my guide recent research that asserts that fantasy is a dimension of reality as valid as the "everyday." Rejecting the idea that popular literature is always politically and morally conservative as well as uniquely promoted by consumerism and media manipulation—although the latter has not hurt Sagan's popularity—I will look at what is healthy in the escapism fundamental to her prose fiction and plays.[3]

I will further examine her popularity as that of a writer who tells an important story of our patriarchal culture, whose texts not only signal a woman at work but also treat women's experiences and perceptions, and whose fantasies inform us of the constraints of a male-dominated society. Sagan's rejection of the "happy ending," her thematic insistence on solitude, her narrators' persistent bittersweet comments, among other aspects of her work, have urged me to bring my own concerns as a feminist to the latent meaning of her texts. I have chosen, then, a reading strategy that uncovers the hidden and critical stance of her romances and also shows how in her plays she disrupts encoded notions of the family and of bourgeois morality.

Sagan is neither a Utopian thinker nor a reformist writer. She does not wave a feminist banner nor does she purport to reinvent language or to speak outside the phallogocentric structure. But, from the plucky and perverse heroine of *Bonjour Tristesse* to the resigned one of *Aimez-vous Brahms . . . .* , from the intense identification established with the fragmented hero/ine of *Un orage immobile* to the satire leveled at misguided masculinity in *Un peu de soleil dans l'eau froide,* she does see lucidly woman's place in patriarchy. She also creates tensions in the depiction of this reality that indicate how literary conventions have reinforced women's limits. And in her short stories in *Musiques de scènes,* she invents Amazons and Avengers who transcend the boundaries of gender.

With scant exceptions, there have been few good readings of Françoise Sagan and almost no revisionary or feminist ones.[4] Her best critics have stressed the escapist element in her works, only to place her among those "contemporary lotus eaters" who have removed themselves from the terrifying complexities of life in an atomic age.[5] No scholar has attempted to understand the enduring phenomenon she represents. With this book I hope to begin to fill these lacunae and also elicit other serious readings of her work. Whether the reader changes his or her praxis after contact with Sagan's fleeting love fantasies is obviously and rightfully out of my control. I expect, however, that her often subtle practice of narrative voicing, her psychological acuity, her seemingly effortless creation of ambience, and her ability to send up in ingenuous parodies not only other popular genres but also herself will not go unappreciated. I add, finally, that my own plot summaries (preceding each discussion of her works) and translations have attempted to do justice to what might best be called an artfully charming style and a playful mastery of the French language.

Judith Graves Miller

University of Wisconsin–Madison

Acknowledgments

I wish to thank Elaine Marks who put a good flea in several ears; the publishing houses of Jean-Jacques Pauvert, Juillard, Flammarion, Gallimard, and E. P. Dutton; John Kaiser of the Penn State library; the feminist scholars and critics who have helped me rethink how to read; my friends and colleagues who have listened, commented, discussed, and cared; the field editor for the Twayne series, David O'Connell, and the general editor, Anne Jones, for their useful suggestions; and Françoise Sagan herself, whose fantasies have inspired me to understand my own.

Chronology

1963   *La Robe mauve de Valentine,* play, performed at Ambassadeurs Theater. Screenplays for *La Recréation* and *Landru.* Divorced from Robert Westhoff.

1964   *Bonheur, impair et passe,* play, performed at Edouard VII Theater. *Toxique,* autobiographical musings. *Château en Suède,* film.

1965   *La Chamade,* novel. Writes legal column in *Nouvel Observateur.*

1966   *Mirror of Venus,* photographs by Wingate Paine, words by Sagan and Frederico Fellini. *L'Echange d'un regard,* ballet for Jacques Chazot. *Le Cheval évanoui* and *L'Echarde,* plays, performed at Gymnase Theater.

1968   *Le Garde du coeur,* novel. *Le Cheval évanoui,* play, moves to Ambassadeurs Theater; *Château en Suède,* play, reopens at Atelier Theater.

1969   *Un peu de soleil dans l'eau froide,* novel. Two films: *La Chamade* and *The Heartkeeper.* Writes lyrics for Jane Fonda and Jeanne Moreau.

1970   *Un piano dans l'herbe,* play, performed at Atelier Theater.

1971   Adaptation of Tennessee Williams's *Sweet Bird of Youth* performed at Atelier Theater. Writes title song for *Un peu de soleil dans l'eau froide,* film.

1972   *Des bleus à l'âme,* autobiographical novel.

1973   *Il est des parfums,* with G. Hanoteau. Pope Paul VI cites Sagan as example of irreligiousity.

1974   *Un profil perdu,* novel. *Réponses,* interviews. *Le Cheval évanoui,* play, reopens at Ambassadeurs Theater. Writes pro-Mitterand editorials.

1975   *Brigitte Bardot racontée par Françoise Sagan, vue par Ghislain Dussart.*

1976   *Des yeux de soie,* short stories. *Encore un hiver,* screenplay and direction by Sagan; *Les Fougères bleus,* screenplay and direction by Sagan, never released.

1977   *Le Lit défait,* novel. First appearance (with Roland Barthes) on "Apostrophes," popular television literary program.

1978   *Le Sang doré des Borgia,* scenario for television film. *Il fait beau jour et nuit,* play, performed at Champs-Elysées Theater.

1979   *Encore un hiver* wins Chris at New York Film Festival. Serves as president of jury, Cannes film festival, and protests that jury was pressured to vote for Coppola's *Apocalypse Now.*

1980   *Le Chien couchant,* novel. Accused and cleared of plagiarism charges relating to *Le Chien couchant.* Trip to Japan where Sagan is proclaimed "symbol of liberty." "Lettre d'amour à Jean-Paul Sartre" first published in *l'Egoïste;* starts seeing Sartre regularly.

1981   *Musiques de scènes,* short stories. *La Femme fardée,* novel. Joins support committee for "Mitterand for President."

1983   *Un orage immobile,* novel.

1984   *Avec mon meilleur souvenir,* memoirs, receives the *Lire* prize for one of twenty best books of 1984.

1985   Article in *Le Monde* satirizing turncoat socialists. *La Maison de Raquel Véga,* short fiction. *De guerre lasse,* novel. Wins Prix de Monaco for the entirety of her work. Preface to *Sand et Musset: Lettres d'amour.*

1987   *Un sang d'aquarelle,* novel. *L'Excès contraire,* play, performed at the Bouffes Parisiens. *Sarah Bernhardt: Le Rire incassable,* biography. *De guerre lasse,* film.

Chapter One
Life and Myth
La Sagan

In the most lyrical essay of the ten that comprise her 1983 memoirs *Avec mon meilleur souvenir (With Fondest Regards)*, Françoise Sagan equates speeding in a sleek sports car with life: "the person who hasn't felt his body become alert, his right hand moving to caress the gears, his left grasping the steering wheel and his legs stretched out, seemingly relaxed but ready for any violent action, for shifting or braking; the person who has not felt, all while executing these attempts at survival, the prestigious and fascinating silence of an imminent death—that mixture of refusal and of provocation death offers us—has never loved speed nor has he ever loved life. . . ."[1] The author has by all accounts—her own and those of myriad commentators—been "loving life," racing through existence, living hard, and risking literal and figurative confrontations with mortality ever since the publication of *Bonjour Tristesse* in 1954. She has become a legend and been caught in the myth of herself: a feminine dandy, a chic and irreplaceable public figure, a neo-romantic gaily and elegantly transforming her despair into art.[2]

If there is such a creature as the "real" Sagan, a being independent of the legendary and paradoxically timid high-roller, the author Sagan rarely hints at her existence. The "Sagan" she presents in her autobiographical writings—*Toxique (Toxique,* 1964); *Des bleus à l'âme (Scars on the Soul,* 1972); and *Avec mon meilleur souvenir (With Fondest Regards,* 1983)—may laugh at some of the excesses of the media portrait, but she also enhances the characterization by colorful and often intriguing illustrations of the character traits the press loves to cite. Sagan has further confused the issue of life and art by producing fiction whose glamorous heroines, frequently her own age, have romantic adventures not unlike some of her own.[3] In addition, by insisting on carrying out her "real" life in exactly the way she chooses, she cultivates the collec-

1

tive fantasy that enjoys seeing her naturalness and sense of adventure as extensions of her protagonists' carefree personalities.

Thus the pursuit of truth in biographical writing turns out to be, in the instance of Françoise Sagan, even more elusive than ever. What follows attempts to identify the salient components and key moments of her life to date, re-create the cultural climate in which the Sagan legend emerged, discuss the conflation of her life and legend through the mid-1980s, and introduce, within this context, her writing.

Prelude to *Bonjour Tristesse* (1935–54)

The region of southwestern France known as the Lot, after the struggling river that flows through it, produces corn, tobacco, pugnacious wine, and an impression of emptiness. Deserted hamlets stand out from the rocky hillsides while bats fly low in the night sky of other, still-inhabited villages. Françoise Quoirez, eventually to become Françoise Sagan, born on her mother's side into a family of comfortable provincial gentry, remembers both the haunted feeling of her birthplace Cajarc and the imperious nature of the grandmother, Mme Laubard, who insisted that Mme Quoirez return from Paris to the Lot in 1935 to deliver Françoise in the bed where she, also, had been born.

Françoise "Sagan," who adopted the pseudonym shortly before her nineteenth birthday in homage to Proust's Duchess, recalls enraptured hours spent reading in her grandparents' attic during summer vacations: "I began [Proust's *Albertine disparue*] and fell to my knees afterwards in a state of sorrow and disillusionment drawn out to a pitch of madness inexorably reexamined, commented upon, probed by the narrator" (*S,* 212); "I discovered that the human being was my only quarry, the only one that interested me, the only one I would never catch, but that I would believe I had touched, perhaps, once in a while . . ." (*S,* 231). Cajarc and her grandparents' home introduced Sagan to literature—her great passion. This secret initiation to a literary vocation and the village with its childhood memories were and remain for her an unspoiled haven, a reminder of roots and rootedness in an otherwise topsy-turvy life.

The period 1935–45 was in anyone's perspective an unsettled and unsettling time in Europe. The triumph in the mid-1930s of fascism in Spain, Italy, and Germany and the rise and fall of the socialist Popular Front in France might not have cast any momentous shadows on Sagan's pleasant existence as a tomboy child of wealthy and charming parents. However, in 1940, after returning from the front of France's brief "phoney" war against Germany, Sagan's father, a prominent industrialist, moved his family from their apartment in Paris's genteel seventeenth *arrondissement* to a country house in the supposed "free" zone outside of Lyons. He had hoped by this disruption to spare his wife and three children the hardships and brutalities of the Occupation. The chosen region, on the contrary, became a center of Resistance activity and, consequently, of relentless German surveillance.

Although Sagan has characteristically made light of the frequent strafings in the fields near her home in Saint Marcellin or the air raids in Lyons where the family also had an apartment, she has nonetheless depicted the grotesqueness of an SS interrogation as a result of her family's aid to a Resistance fighter. She has also reported her uncomprehending distress after the Liberation at the sight of the shaven and tar covered women humiliated by local patriots for their romantic involvement with German soldiers. Moreover, like many French children of her generation, she watched and absorbed the horror of the first newsreel from the concentration camp at Dachau, a film that was unconscionably coupled with the light-hearted Saturday movie matinee.

Despite a certain fragility (which even now characterizes her appearance, if not anymore her constitution), Sagan actively savored the years in Saint Marcellin and, especially, the opportunities afforded by the township's lush surroundings. She learned to love nature, swimming, animals, and challenging hikes in the countryside. She also learned, at least retrospectively, that these pleasures are frequently only superficial accompaniments to the reality of an ongoing terror.

After the family reclaimed its Parisian apartment in 1945, Sagan continued the audacious excursions begun in Saint Marcellin. But this time she took emotional as well as physical risks. Her unorthodox, often uncooperative behavior as a Parisian school girl resulted in withdrawal or expulsion from a series of private and religious establishments. Her pranks caused her to be thrown out of the plush private school of Louise de Bettignies, and she hid the situation from her parents for several months in order to spend her days taking the bus to the Place de la Concorde where she read novels on the quay overlooking the Seine. She was dismissed on the spot from the Couvent des Oiseaux when she recited Jacques Prévert's poem, "Life is a little bird." Her teachers were appalled by her lack of piety and, especially, her pleasure in emphasizing the verse "Our father who art in Heaven, why don't you stay there?"

If iconoclastic, disrespectful, and untamed, Sagan was also extremely bright and a much-admired student, particularly for her sensitivity to literature. At the Cours Hattemer, where she prepared her *baccalauréat* exams, her intellectual precociousness drew the attention of classmate Florence Malraux, with whom she was to wile away countless afternoons in innumerable cafés discussing contemporary writers, including the latter's celebrated father. Contact with the Malraux entourage, which with the equally influential Sartrean group, signaled and consecrated most literary trends throughout the 1950s, suggested to Sagan how to go about publishing her own writings. To this end, Colette Audry, then a collaborator on Sartre's *Les Temps modernes,* was of crucial assistance.

By 1952, enrolled in a preparatory program for literary studies at the Sorbonne, Sagan had already written a number of short stories. She had also, and not less felicitously for her writing career, discovered the jazz clubs of Saint Germain des Prés. She thus began to partake of the multitude of enchantments that had become a maelstrom for the intense and turbulent postwar generation, a generation of which she would soon find herself heralded the "spokesperson." True to form, in June 1953, Sagan failed her entrance exams to the Sorbonne, having spent far more time sipping cognac, palavering, and dancing than studying. She consequently made up her mind to devote the rest of the summer to finishing *Bonjour Tristesse,* the novel that was to become France's greatest postwar literary sensation.

Bonjour Tristesse and the Creation of the Legend

François Mauriac, esteemed novelist, great-uncle of French letters, and defender of the Catholic faith, could not fail to comment when an eighteen-year-old girl's first novel, in which the teenaged narrator loses her virginity, causes the tragic demise of her father's affair, and gets away with both, won the coveted Prix des Critiques in May 1954. Calling Sagan "a charming monster" and a "shocking little girl," he praised her talent while deploring her lack of spiritual commitment.[4] Nearly twenty-two pounds[5] of less-quoted journal and newspaper articles echo not only Mauriac's concern with the novel's "amorality," but also his fascination with its creator and ultimately with the public's enthusiastic response: the publisher René Julliard easily sold over

850,000 copies of *Bonjour Tristesse* within the first three months of its appearance. By the early 1960s, *Bonjour Tristesse* had been translated into twenty-three languages. Its sales exceeded four million copies. The novel's success catapulted Sagan into the unreliable limelight of the popular and even not-so-popular press where she has, with the minor falls from grace of a "Liz Taylor," "the Kennedys," and "the British Royals," remained ever since. In fact, her novels and plays have rarely sold fewer and usually more than 150,000 copies each, in a country where books that sell 50,000 copies are considered tremendous best-sellers.

The immediate effect of *Bonjour Tristesse* was to establish Sagan, by the winter of 1955, as the darling of le Tout Paris—that vortex of publishers, journalists, entertainers, artists, stylists, and assorted jet-setters who determine, with the help of the media, what is "in." Likewise, the Tout New York made her the toast of the town during her visit there in the spring of 1956.[6] Her renown was such that Russian poet Yevgeny Yevtushenko, on his trip to Paris in 1963, listed her as the number one person he wished to meet. Brigitte Bardot was number two.

That Brigitte Bardot ranked right behind Sagan in Yevtushenko's mind might help posit an answer to why the publication of *Bonjour Tristesse* caused such a furor. Sagan herself has proposed on several occasions that the fact that her narrator-heroine Cécile could make love, enjoy it, and not have to pay at the end of the novel by a clandestine abortion or a hasty marriage both shocked the reigning moral order and spoke to the overwhelming need of young people to throw off the shackles of sexual oppression. Bardot's frank and unashamed sensuality in, for example, *And God Created Woman,* the 1956 film that introduced her, literally fleshed out this right to physical pleasure. The new morality, with its emphasis on leisure and self-indulgence represented by Bardot as well as Sagan, undoubtedly spoke to the unarticulated desires of burgeoning adults, young women in particular, sick of the deprivations of the 1939–44 conflict, reluctant to give in to the anguish of the cold war, and repulsed by a code of morality gone bankrupt through the wartime experiences of the 1940s.

It is not insignificant, either, that both Sagan and Bardot hailed from upper middle-class Right Bank families. The Left Bank, with its Saint-Germain-des-Prés intellectuals, night spots, and café life had, after the Occupation, already espoused liberation in its many forms.

Until the mid-1950s, however, this older generation, including writers such as Sartre, de Beauvoir, Camus, and Vian, was considered by the staid bourgeoisie to be bohemian, marginal, and not an inside threat to the continuation of the social hierarchy and dominant morality. Sagan, unlike her seniors, never rejected her status as a member of the bourgeoisie, was recognized as one of its own, and yet still made a point of tolling the death knell of such unalterable bourgeois values as inherited position, the sacredness of the patriarchal family, and the primacy of duty.

The plethora of photographs taken of Sagan in the first few years following the stunning reception of *Bonjour Tristesse* always project this same contradictory image. In one of the two favored poses, Sagan, dressed in a tailored gray skirt and dark cashmere turtleneck, "at home" in a well-appointed bourgeois interior, reaches toward a half-empty bottle of Scotch, cigarette in hand. In the second typical shot, Sagan, a fresh-faced innocent waif, speeds away in a Jaguar, on top of a motor launch, or on a race horse. The camera communicates how she stretches decorum and the accepted order by her penchant for American-style whisky, chain smoking, and an unrelenting personal rhythm. Yet the adherence to the conservative uniform of upper middle-class girls, the familiarity with period furniture, and the ingenuousness of the impish face communicate something of the "dutiful daughter" whose world coheres formally in ways embraced by the bourgeois community.

This slight young woman heretically enjoyed impressing on everyone's mind that she truly adored fast cars, Johnny Walker Black Label, and independence. To borrow one of Sagan's favorite words of praise, these almost "virile" qualities aroused hysterical criticism from magazines such as *Marie-Claire* that attacked her absence of femininity, her morality, and—the color of her carpet.[7]

Many other critics, most of them erstwhile novelists or preachers treating "the case of Sagan" as a podium, tried in the five-year aftermath of *Bonjour Tristesse* to explain the phenomenon of the novel's success.[8] Certain Catholic essayists, echoing Mauriac who continued to depict Sagan's consciousness of evil, used the novel to launch their own diatribes about the terrifying immorality of non-Christians. They abhorred the nonbeliever's need to resort to frivolity to fill up his or her time and condemned the "profound sadness" of Sagan's Godless, structureless universe.[9] Others understood her novel as a logical development in existential literature. For them, Sagan's world embodied the void of human existence without prescribing redemptive action. In this perspective Sagan became the symbol of a generation looking for a way to live while accepting as a given life's emptiness.[10] Commentaries about Sagan's text, as well as about her life, have almost exclusively neglected her talents as a writer in order to promote this legend of the "poor little lost girl."

Mestastases of the legend—Sagan: the restless spirit, the daredevil, the hedonist, the spendthrift—along with its attendant newsworthiness and publicity value have managed to endure through the Algerian War, the "absurd" theater of Ionesco, Beckett, and Genet, television, astrophysicists' dreams of putting a man on the moon, the New Novel, New Wave films, sixties rock music and the Americanization of French culture, the social revolution of May 1968, feminism, collective creations, the repercussions of the revelations of the Soviet Gulag, and five French presidents. In 1971 when, with such important authors as Marguerite Duras, Simone de Beauvoir, Alain Robbe-Grillet, and Jean-Paul Sartre, Sagan had part of a book translated into slang for an anthology called *l'Académie d'Argot* (The academy of slang), the newspaper, *Le Figaro,* chose to highlight *her* text in its advertisements. Her name alone would guarantee good sales. And in 1979, in a poll taken by *Paris-Match,* readers placed Sagan among the top eleven well-known Frenchwomen. She was the only writer to make the chart. Certain journalists have conferred on her the aura of sainthood or, perhaps, martyrdom. As recently as 1984, Patrick Poivre d'Arvor gushed, for example: "Sagan is still magical. Yesterday, when she gave me the only copy of her book to have left the Gallimard printers' hands, I touched it as though it were a holy relic."[11]

The emphasis on her mythic status has evolved from the "charming but naughty young girl" to the "forever charming but somewhat world-weary (if best-dressed), literary figure."[12] However, the publication of every new novel, play, or volume of short stories provokes reflections that continue to harken back to the iconic status of Sagan's first work. While she has published over thirty-three titles, plus sundry articles on travel and fashion, scenarios for film and television, lyrics to songs, and even a personal report on the first anniversary of the Cuban Revolution, critics and journalists find in the earliest prose the inspiration for their analyses. "La Sagan" is inseparable from the novel that inaugurated her career. The title of the latest, and this time intelligent, photobiography—Bertrand Poirot-Delpech's *Bonjour Sagan*[13]—speaks to the durability of the original voice.

Variations on a Theme (1955–86)

"I've led an agitated existence, a life of peripeteia, God only knows why! I'm impulsive. I like clamor and craziness. I often can't control myself."[14] In dozens of interviews—over fourscore of which have been collected in *Réponses (Nightbird,* 1974)[15]—Sagan has clearly had fun confirming the inoperable fusion between the Sagan persona and the private person. Like Jean Genet, she has adopted the posture that others have imposed on her and has been teasingly reinforcing this image ever since: "I have worn my legend like a veil. This delightful mask, somewhat over-simplified, correspond[s] to certain of my obvious tastes: speed, the sea, midnight, everything explosive, everything dark, everything ephemeral . . ." (*R,* 12). Her post-1954 personal history does, indeed, inscribe itself within this glittery but also perilous frame.

Until the mid-1970s Sagan had been a regular among the nocturnal fauna that make and break the Parisian night-club circuit. With her brother Jacques, model Annabel Schwob de Lure, painter Bernard Buffet, writer Bernard Frank, composer Michel Magne, singer Juliette Gréco, professional man-about-town Jacques Chazot, hostess Régine, and a shifting crowd of reporters, artists, and actors, Sagan animated in the 1950s and 1960s such Parisian night spots as the Club du Vieux Colombier and the Tête de l'Art. A tear gas bomb in May 1968 tossed through the open door of New Jimmy's found her helping Régine evacuate the wounded to the private apartment located over the club. She lived through many of the convolutions of the 1960s and 1970s in this indirectly involved and, in the last analysis, mostly detached fashion. Her excesses on the social scene, however, eventually caught up with her, and in the mid-1970s she stopped drinking in order to retrieve her health and her sanity.

Sagan has not glittered only in an already sparkling capital city. In 1955, she and her brother rented a villa at La Ponche, a sleepy fishing port on the Mediterranean. The carefree group of Parisian personalities known as "Sagan's gang," along with associated pals the likes of Roger Vadim, Brigitte Bardot, Jean-Louis Trintignant, and filmmaker Alexandre Astruc, noisily cavorted that summer and in over a dozen following summers on the beaches, in the waves, and in the proliferating night clubs of the region, thereby helping create, to Sagan's later dismay, the cult of Saint-Tropez. These summers, however, also solidified her friendship and her connections with the art and fashion establishment whose support turns every premiere of her plays and ballets into social events of the first magnitude.

Sagan has known myriad disasters and victories related to her fast-paced existence. In April 1957, on her way to the still paradisiacal Saint-Tropez for a needed change from a drizzly Parisian spring, she rolled her Aston Martin, flipping the car four times: she broke eleven ribs, smashed her legs and fractured her skull. A priest administered the last rites, but when she did not die, indignant editorials hinted that she deserved what she got.

Hospitalized all that summer, she suffered so terribly she considered killing herself. She recovered, however, at the price of becoming addicted to the morphine-based painkiller that helped her relearn how to walk. In *Toxique* (1964), a remarkable confession of her detoxification cure, Sagan, presaging Marguerite Duras through the medium of Yann Andréa's *MD*, allows herself to be seen in the ugly, uncontrollable, and very private abyss of the addict. Bernard Buffet's stark and distorted line drawings, which accompany the text, give form to the fragmented consciousness that Sagan courageously pulled back together.

This brush with death and loss of self may have helped precipitate in 1958 her first marriage to publisher Guy Schoeller, a man twenty-one years her senior. They divorced within two years, Sagan citing as emblematic of their differences his closet with its many pairs of perfectly aligned shoes. In 1962 she married again. Her new husband, American-born Bob Westhoff, fathered Sagan's one child Denis, and lived with mother and son until 1970, even though he and Sagan were divorced in 1963. Sagan has never thought that marriage had much to do with loving a man. Since the breakup of her relationship to Westhoff, who is still a friend, she has changed escorts only slightly less frequently than apartments, cars, and publishers.

Perhaps her compulsive gambling captures more than anything else the spirit that disallows any settling down. Her passion for roulette, while providing her in 1959 with the necessary sum of money to buy a spacious and well-loved home in Normandy—her one stable possession—also forced her in 1966 to demand her own banishment from all gaming tables in France. Gambling for Sagan, in much the same way as she characterizes speeding, means forgetting about "the passing of time, the weight of money, and society's tentacular hold" (*S*, 36), but, of course, it also means risking everything that one owns. In the mid-1960s, Sagan could no longer risk that everything because she had a son, numerous pets, and several friends to support. Of these friends she has noted with a mixture of melancholy and tenderness: "It often happens that I prefer these weaker sorts to the so-called superior types, uniquely because of that compunction which directs them to hurl themselves, like fireflies or night moths, against the four corners of the giant lampshade of life."[16]

Besides motherhood and friendship, which have suited her very well, Sagan has made other commitments that belie a life of superficial extravagance. She has never, for example, renounced her opposition to French imperialism. She signed, in 1960, the "Petition of the 121" which demanded that unwilling draftees be accorded the right to defect from the French army during the Algerian War. For this and her vocal support of Algerian independence, the ultraconservative Organisation Armée Secrète (OAS) bombed her apartment. She joined with other famous and less famous Frenchwomen in 1971 to demonstrate in favor of state-subsidized abortion on demand and, in a move that could have resulted in incarceration for all the signatories, added her name to those who claimed they had had illegal abortions in the past. She has also continuously championed the socialism of François Mitterand, publishing a front-page editorial in Le Monde in 1985[17] that satirized turncoat socialists who were deserting the ship of state.

Yet despite these grand and unquestionably serious gestures, she has remained on the outside of any sustained or profoundly thought-out political action. Her feminism, to take one issue, stops with the call for women's rights to control their own bodies and the demand of equal pay for equal work. She has publicly declared her sympathy for men deprived of their power by militant feminists and she refuses any notion of an equalitarian Utopia. She has also joked that part of her socialist activism has consisted in reassuring her rich friends that they do not need to skip the country.

Sagan operates, it would seem, out of instinct and élan, hating the intellectual pretentiousness of many of the fraternity of writers who, according to her, in one variation prescribe political liberation for the ills of the "people" and, in the other, rely on their readers to supply the creativity they cannot dredge up themselves. Her worst nightmare of old age is to find herself on a literary jury with other women writers of her generation—Marguerite Duras, Françoise Mallet-Joris, and Geneviève Dormann—all four resigned to their status as literary *grandes dames.* Humble about her own work, she has said of the tumult caused by her publications: "I am an accident that keeps on happening."[18]

Françoise Sagan: Writer

Sagan's modesty about her writing must not be confused with nonchalance, although critics who do address her style have regularly and avuncularly pointed out her grammatical mistakes, overdependence on adverbs, and redundancies.[19] Commentators have themselves repetitiously employed the catch phrase "her sweet music" as well as other—and tempting—musical metaphors to explain the lure of her prose. What the press has curiously omitted, however, in its surface examination of Sagan the writer, is her own insistence throughout the autobiographical texts on what writing means to her. She has devoted as much time to weaving complicated images or creating tragicomic vignettes of her struggles with the blank page as she has to mulling over her other passions, so much so that an examination of the conclusion "her writing is her life," while itself a bit simplistic, permits a more circumspect reading of the legend.

To begin, both the autobiographical *Des bleus à l'âme* and *Avec mon meilleur souvenir* are fundamentally celebrations of Sagan's rapport with writing. They appear disguised as something else, in the former case another novel of failed romance with authorial digressions, and in the latter a series of remembrances of artists Sagan has admired, as well as sketches of her great obsessions. However, each in its own way illustrates the basic but often overlooked fact that a writer, to paraphrase Barthes, writes. Or, to parody Descartes: "Sagan writes, therefore she is." She has said as much in an unusually earnest moment in 1977: "Writing is the only proof I have of my self, to my eyes it is the only tangible sign that I exist."[20]

In *Des bleus à l'âme,* Sagan meanderingly portrays her writing as therapeutic for both herself and her readers. The author skillfully juxtaposes in one tight volume the story of Eléonore and Sébastien Van Milhem with the elucubrations of her authorial persona speaking, while at the same time composing the brother's and sister's adventure. The Van Milhems, golden Scandinavians whose incestuous affections and peculiar complicity had already powered Sagan's fiction twelve years earlier in the play *Château en Suède,* return in the "novel" part of the double text. In the novel's Parisian setting, they offer their charms, in the sumptuously disinterested fashion that is their trademark, in exchange for protection. A third-person narrator recounts various episodes in their desultory quest for the next "patron."

The authorial persona, who we might call "F. S.," interrupts the narration at various points to establish the second level of the text: both a writer's diary and a series of ruminations on life in contemporary France. In this part, F. S. complains about, among other things, the omnipresent violence in Paris, her terrible disenchantment with French selfishness, political militants' mania for suppressing individualism, and everybody's failure to live without drugging their sensibilities.

The writer's diary, of greater interest here than the novel, plays with many of the familiar critical barbs tossed at Sagan, such as "not enough scenery," "too few details," or "too much of the same leisured milieu," and neutralizes them by a conscious self-parody. F. S. also explains how her imagination works and how she writes. This Woody Allen–like persona seduces the reader by establishing a feeling of immediacy that seems to pull him or her directly into the writer's mind. For example, as soon as the third-person narrator introduces into the fiction of Eléonore and Sébastien in chapter 3 an unidentified character, the authorial persona F. S. bursts onto the scene, admitting that she does not know what to do with him. So she drops him from her fiction.

By the end of the double text, the attentive reader understands that Eléonore and Sébastien represent more than fabulous actors, aristocratic bohemians, or perverse opportunists. They are glorious foils against each other's solitude, but they are also extensions of the authorial persona F. S. and therefore a foil for her, too. Indeed, in chapter 14, Eléonore and F. S. indistinguishably share the narrative's point of view. And in a Pirandellian transformation in the final chapter, the authorial persona F. S. becomes the first-person narrator of the "novel," taking over the job of the original third-person narrator and also establishing herself as a character in her own right. F. S. then meets Eléonore and Sébastien in the streets of Paris and invites them to her house in Normandy where they can all lick their wounds.

Where is the fiction then? Which are the fictional characters? What are fiction's limits? From the beginning, a suicidal menace has hung over both parts of the double text: the "novel"and the writer's digressions. The authorial persona F. S., however, saves herself, for she kills off in the "novel" Robert Bessy, Eléonore's and Sébastien's latest gull. In this way F. S. makes use of another fictional alter ego to end the misery of life which she, herself, cannot bring to a close.

To return to the "unidentified character" in chapter 3, F. S. reintroduces him in chapter 17 and then shuns him as an outsider, the one who, in opposition to the already-involved reader, cannot creep into the fiction. He cannot, like Eléonore and Sébastien, or like F. S., or like the reader during the time of the reading, turn his life into art. He cannot escape from the humdrum "métro, boulot, dodo"[21] that characterizes the average daily existence.

F. S., however, can escape and, in spite of the suicide of Robert Bessy, work through the mood of melancholy that dominates *Des bleus à l'âme* to a moment of hope, arrested by the ray of sunlight at the book's close. Writing, then, protects F. S. and by extrapolation the author herself. In *Des bleus à l'âme,* Sagan directly transforms her emotional life into fiction.

While *Des bleus à l'âme* can be read as an attempt to resolve a personal crisis, *Avec mon meilleur souvenir,* beautifully orchestrated in ten movements of measured prose, reads like a meditation. The mood varies from essay to essay across a limited and tender spectrum. It ranges from nostalgia in the first piece on jazz singer Billie Holiday, to self-mocking dramatization in "Saint-Tropez," to charmed admiration in the much remarked upon "Lettre d'amour à Jean-Paul Sartre." Ironically inscribed within this controlled and sculpted form, the central concern emerges as a fascination with the outsized, the flamboyant, the totally absorbing. This preoccupation unites the diverse activities: gambling, speeding, rehearsing, relaxing, reading and the various personalities Sagan offers the readers—Holiday, Tennessee Williams, Orson Welles, Rudolf Nureyev, and Sartre. Whether the passion she exalts be the sea or sports cars, whether she recalls the anecdote of Billie Holiday's needle-marked arms or Orson Welles's monstrous genius, Sagan's subjects share the same emotional profile: unmediated, impassioned, unafraid. Each remembered risk, each memorialized artist merges in a fully engaged combat with the limits of the human condition. Speeding or Sartre both speak to living one's solitude aggressively. Gambling and Billie Holiday both evoke the intoxication of the fine line between absolute freedom and absolute collapse.

It is more than appropriate that Sagan chooses to cap all the essays in this volume by a reader's autobiography, a promenade through the texts that have formed her as a writer: Gide's *The Fruits of the Earth,* Camus's *The Rebel,* Rimbaud's *Illuminations,* and especially Proust's *Remembrance of Things Past.* No less meaningful is the thrill that literature has always provoked in her: "Since Rimbaud's *Illuminations,* literature

has constantly made me feel there was a fire someplace—everywhere—
and that it was up to me to put it out" (S, 209). All the earlier essays
hint that her various enthusiasms are but permutations of this ultimate
one. She thus equates the furor and necessity of gambling with the
excitement of the opening of a new play, and indicates that passing
behemoth trucks on the highway calls for the same psychological stam-
ina as discovering the endless complexity of the writer's basic matter—
humankind.

The penultimate essay, Sagan's radiant remembrance of Sartre, again
serves to present her as the ever-grateful daughter of "the words": Sartre
and Sagan, connected by the same birthday, by their fearlessness of big
emotions, by their incapacity to live any other way than as though
there were no tomorrow. The authors are connected, too, and this is
Sagan's point in writing these memoirs, by the writer's passion, a passion that in Sagan's case both personalizes and intensifies her legendary
heroes while setting her forth as one of their number.

Life as Theater

The way in which Sagan lives and the place of her writing within
that life evidence a conscious or, perhaps, unconscious choice to thea-
tricalize existence in order to make life less burdensome and less predictable. Theatricalization protects her against the awful cruelty of the
contemporary world, the feeling she has often mentioned of accelerat-
ing toward a disaster over which she has no control. Thus her supposed
frivolousness might be considered an act of personal freedom. Her dan-
dyism, her moral decency, her physical elegance would be a way of
giving shape to a sense of absence. She is a French Peggy Lee singing,
"If that's all there is, then let's keep dancing," and a female Noël Coward engineering a massive seduction of her audience by her style and
her humor. Sagan may call it quits with metaphysical and political
meaning, but she gives meaning, nonetheless, because she gives form.
Gallimard, the pinnacle of French publishers, has obviously recognized
the value of her particular contribution to French letters by inviting
her, as of 1983, into its fold, an invitation, according to Philippe
Sollers, tantamount to becoming a prime investment commodity of the
National Bank.[22]

Sagan's star status, which propels her out of society, also reflects the
public's projection of its own freedom. Stars, including star storytell-
ers, encourage the "lesser mortals" by producing desire—desire to keep

life going, desire, when the stars are makers of tales, to hear more. Antoine Blondin, in his 1974 evaluation of her work, suggests that Sagan gives to life's most fugitive pleasures the value that, in their heart of hearts, most people place upon them as well: "The captivating quality of what has been rather grotesquely called 'the famous little voice' and what is [in fact] her style and her tone, comes from the marvelous precision of an instrument that de-banalizes the real."[23]

Chapter Two

Perversions of the Family Romance in First-Person Narratives

Sagan and the Romance

Françoise Sagan writes romances, that is, novels whose narratives concern themselves with the coming together and/or breaking apart of that compelling entity "a man and a woman." This rather contemporary definition of romance places it within the purview of other forms of popular literature which, as John Cawelti notes: "guarantee the fulfillment of conventional expectations."[1] Created to give enjoyment, romances traditionally follow the vicissitudes of a love relationship and end in marriage. More recent romances, however, tend to concentrate on the failure of marriage or the couple and end by a splitting asunder. Sagan's romances, on the whole, conform to the latter pattern.

Earlier considerations of romance, such as the understanding of the genre as primarily an inward quest, also apply to her fiction and complement the view of romance as merely "postures of yearning, pleasing, choosing, slipping, falling, and failing."[2] While indeed falling in or out of love, Sagan's protagonists are also searching, sometimes unconsciously, for something beyond the promise of a love affair. Moreover, if in many ways conventional, Sagan's romances also call forth a reading that goes uncomfortably against the grain of the traditional love story.

The Saganian romance possesses certain characteristics that, present from novel to novel (with rare exceptions),[3] constitute the fictional universe within which and out of which she weaves her love affair. The time frame is contemporary, with the love story developing chronologically from beginning to end, often as a year-long saga. The milieu is moneyed and usually Parisian—a world of leisure but also of fast-paced alluring professions: journalism, advertising, fashion, publishing. Work, per se, is never an issue. And the intimacy of home yields to the promiscuity of night clubs, rented apartments, or hotel rooms.

16

While the true protagonist is most often female, Sagan's novels will usually concentrate on two or three main characters, male and female. A trio is more prevalent where the triangular intrigue—always present in some form even if disguised—takes narrative precedence over the love duo. Ranging in age from almost twenty to just about fifty, Sagan's characters elicit the epithet "splendid human specimens." No babies, children, or old people mar the physiognomic landscape. From three to a half-dozen secondary figures make brief appearances; frequently one of this supporting group will prove a catalyst, effecting encounters between the lovers.

About a third of each novel is given over to jaunty scenes of dialogue that are cleverly interspersed for maximum reader interest within relatively short *récits* (what happens next) and commentaries. Longer and frequent analytical passages, particularly in the earlier novels, reinforce the central concern as one of character and interpersonal rapport rather than of action or setting. The story is flawlessly articulated, building through a causal chain to an inevitable ending, generally foreseen from the first chapter. However, if the closing meets the reader's expectations, it is, as mentioned previously, practically never the "happy ever after" ending of the formulaic Harlequin or Silhouette romance.

Finally, charming and deft imagery, specifically correspondences between the heroine's or hero's emotional state and country or cityscapes, establish the mood. Extended metaphors of natural phenomena or of man-made objects often introduce a note of sadness in the first paragraphs of the normally compact novels or in the beginning paragraphs of several different chapters. And throughout Sagan's work, specific key words—"ennui" (variously: boredom or malaise and moral fatigue), "indifférence" (disconnectedness, lack of involvement), "insouciance" (carefreeness, lack of constraints)—help create and maintain an ambience of pleasurable melancholy. Tone, then, is a major element of a Sagan romance.

In the thirty-odd years of her career and, more exactly, in the composition of her fifteen published novels, Sagan has, as might be expected, modified and somewhat reoriented her treatment of the romance. While most traces of didacticism, moral lessons, or political preoccupations still remain outside the scope of the novels—give or take an occasional aphorism à la Rochefoucauld[4]—the love relationship has at times been displaced from its prime position. Furthermore, Sagan has altered her mode, or her manner of treating her subject. Two distinct and obviously connected modes distinguish the novels prior to 1973 from those written after that date. Using a musical analogy, we

might term the first group "minor" and the second "major." The pre-
1973 or minor mode group—which includes *Bonjour Tristesse* (1954),
Un certain sourire (*A Certain Smile*, 1956), *Dans un mois, Dans un an*
(*Those Without Shadows*, 1957), *Aimez-vous Brahms . . .* , (1959), *Les
Merveilleux nuages* (*The Wonderful Clouds*, 1961), *La Chamade* (1965),
Un peu de soleil dans l'eau froide (*A Few Hours of Sunlight*, 1962), and
Des bleus à l'âme (*Scars on the Soul*, 1972)—is subtler and more ambiguous than the later romances. The point of view of these minor mode
novels is personal, closer to the reader and to the main character. The
story is told by either a first-person narrator/protagonist or third-person narrators who identify their points of view with that of the heroine.
     The post-1973 or major mode group—counting *Le Garde du coeur*
(*The Heartkeeper*, 1968),[5] *Un profil perdu* (*Lost Profile*, 1974), *Le Lit
défait* (*The Unmade Bed*, 1977), *Le Chien couchant* (*Salad Days*, 1980),
Un orage immobile (*The Still Storm*, 1983), *De guerre lasse* (*A Reluctant
Hero*, 1985), and *Un sang d'aquarelle* (Water-color blood, 1987), among
its number—relies on more melodramatic techniques: exaggerated
emotions, an increase in coincidences and surprises, more intricate
plots and even subplots. Usually an impersonal third-person narrator,
a therefore less confessional narrator than that of the first group, tells
the story. In the major mode, there is less probing of what makes
individual characters tick and more emphasis on social satire, a comic
proclivity present in only discrete doses in the earlier novels. In addition, aspects of self-parody or parody of other popular forms infuse
several novels of the post-1973 group with a. delightful tongue-in-
cheek sensibility.
     Within the first or minor mode group, notably in her two earliest
first-person narratives *Bonjour Tristesse* and *Un certain sourire*, Sagan explores the most basic form of the romance, termed by psychoanalysts
the "family romance." Not surprisingly, this "coming of age within
the family" theme structures the novels she wrote when she herself was
an adolescent. Nonetheless, even at this stage in her career she eschews
a traditional treatment of the family and the oedipal drama and begins
to play with the peculiarities of the original love story in ways that
encourage a reading of these first novels as perversions.

The First Love Story: The Family Romance

     Sigmund Freud used the term "family romance" to designate the
unconscious evolution in which a child, through identification with
the same-sexed parent, transfers his or her sexual desire to the opposite

parent. By further displacement of this desire to nonfamily members of the opposite sex, the child enters into society as a gendered subject, on the way to fulfilling a role as "woman" or "man." Feminist rereadings of Freud have recently understood the family romance as not only the psychological process that maintains the family as it is already established, that is male-dominated, but also as a socializing force that reinforces patriarchy in all realms of social and political organization. The family romance is thus seen to perpetuate, to the detriment of women, the sex-gender system, the primary way in which the world is divided and structured.

The plot of the family romance has been variously adapted by novelists, intuitively or consciously, to examine a character's passage from childhood to adulthood—a fictional convention to be sure, since in developmental terms the "Oedipal drama," the crucial locus of the family romance, is played out earlier than adolescence, the usual fictional starting point. Certain psychoanalytic critics, Marthe Robert in particular, argue that the family romance in fact subtends *all* novels.[6] According to her, a character's dilemma, whether it implies decision-making, growth, self-definition, insight, or all of these, always inscribes itself within the pattern of identification with, then distancing from, the parents or parental figures and, finally, reinsertion into society and/or establishment of a new rapport with social or other authority.

For our purposes, the narrower connection between the family romance and a fictional family love story with a quest motif included therein, provides an especially useful entry into Françoise Sagan's first two minor mode novels. Both treat the triangular conflict basic to the family romance. Both follow the heroine's evolution through a sexual initiation to a different awareness of her self. Both also, however, twist and mangle the Freudian psychobiological model considered "healthy" as well as the conventional fictional version of the family meant to ease the young girl's voyage into predictable womanhood.[7] An examination of the functioning of the family romance in *Bonjour Tristesse* and *Un certain sourire* shows how Sagan, in the creation of her fictional oedipal drama, undermines the expected outcome of the family romance plot.

Bonjour Tristesse

Cécile Gets What She Wants. Seventeen-year-old Cécile and her advertising-executive father Raymond, a playboy widower, have left Paris for what is meant to be a carefree vacation on the Riviera in

a secluded villa surrounded by pine forests and the sea. Raymond's redheaded mistress Elsa, a sometimes model, oftimes professional companion, has gone with them. Cécile, soon after cleansing herself of a
year of Parisian dust in the cool waters of the Mediterranean, meets
Cyril, a responsible young man and serious law student. He and his
mother have rented a vacation home nearby. Cyril gamely offers to
teach Cécile how to sail.

In anticipation of her nautical debut, Cécile gives herself over to the
thrills of the evening—shooting stars and crickets' mating calls. Raymond, however, announces the imminent arrival of Anne Larsen, an
old friend of Cécile's long-deceased mother. Anne has also been instru-
mental in helping Cécile adjust to the demands of a sophisticated Parisian world after leaving her provincial convent school. Cécile notes
with some concern that Anne is everything she and her father are not:
self-assured, intellectual, refined, unselfish, kind, controlled—in other
words, adult.

On the day of Anne's arrival, Cyril kisses Cécile for the first time
and awakens in her a violent emotion. Raymond and Elsa, in the mean-
time, have gone to fetch Anne at the train station, but she has preferred
to drive down from Paris in her comfortable American car. Apparently
upset by the news of Elsa's presence, Anne, nevertheless, wins over the
odd family of Raymond, Elsa, and Cécile in the course of their first
evening together.

The swollen and peeling Elsa cannot compete with the svelte, bru-
nette, and subtle Anne, who not only begins to command Raymond's
attentions but also Cécile's life. Discovering that Cécile has failed her
final high school exams, Anne frightens her by suggesting a strict
study regimen. In retaliation, Cécile shocks both Anne and her father
by voicing her outrage at bourgeois conformity after the three of them
take tea with Cyril's very proper, very widowed mother.

The inevitable comes to pass: a well-timed excursion to the gambling casino permits Raymond to escape from Elsa long enough to
negotiate a new couple with Anne. Cécile is given the task of dealing
with any hysterics on Elsa's part. She chooses, instead, to get drunk
and empathize with the sun-burned loser. Oblivious to Cécile's disarray, Raymond and Anne announce their intention of getting married.
Within a week, the "normalized" family (Anne, Raymond, and Cécile)
lurches into motion.

Cyril is especially glad that Cécile will finally have real parents.
However, when Anne stumbles upon the young couple embracing in
the pine forest, she forbids them to see each other again. She then puts

into action her threat to discipline Cécile's study habits. Shut up in her room and faced with the philosopher Bergson's notion of vital energy—an ironic concept given her situation—Cécile realizes she cannot allow Anne to change in this drastic fashion her free and easy life and privileged rapport with her father.

Elsa, now evenly tanned and recovered from sunburn if not heartburn, comes back to reclaim her suitcases. Cécile is at home alone. Seeing the luscious and youthful Elsa, Cécile devises on the spot a plan to disrupt or, better, halt altogether Anne and Raymond's marriage. She will manipulate both Elsa and Cyril and, by addressing herself to their self-interests—Elsa's desire to have Raymond back and Cyril's love—she will wreak havoc between Raymond and Anne. In a secret meeting, she convinces her two willing guinea pigs to play at being lovers. Knowing her father as she does, Cécile wagers that he will not be able to resist making a jealous pass at Elsa.

Although Cécile debates with herself on several different occasions about her own lack of ethics, she never manages to confront Anne openly with her anger and frustration. Furthermore, Anne resists or deters at the last minute any chance for real communication between them. She thus hampers the possibility of effecting a reversal of Cécile's plans. After one final humiliating scene with Anne, Cécile runs off to Cyril to make love for the first time. She will thereafter frequently find solace for her squeaky conscience in his arms.

While Cécile basks hypocritically in Anne's sympathy over the difficult situation of having to watch her ex-boyfriend squire about Elsa, her machinations advance. Cyril and Elsa regularly sail around the promontory performing their affection for each other before Raymond's nonplussed eyes. They pretend to tryst in the pine forest, conveniently cuddling at the moment when Raymond and Cécile stroll by. They show up at the Saint Raphael night club where Raymond, Anne, and Cécile are spending an embarrassing evening with some vulgar acquaintances who cannot stop jabbering about Elsa's attractions.

The inevitable happens again. Raymond cedes to temptation. Anne, somewhat suspicious, discovers him and Elsa together in the pine forest. Completely undone, she flees in her car and, later that day, drives off the road at the most dangerous spot on the highway. Her death—or her suicide—leaves Raymond and Cécile alone. The tragedy separates all the various love combinations except that of father and daughter who nurse each other and their unhappiness back to a state of tolerable sadness in Paris.

Reading the Family Romance in *Bonjour Tristesse*. As just recounted, the plot of *Bonjour Tristesse* introduces certain of the components of Sagan's first "altered" family romance. Unusual both in terms of the orthodox psychoanalytical model and in terms of the conventional fictional family romance, *Bonjour Tristesse* presents a sexual initiation, but the concurrent acceptance of the gendered role and the resulting socially correct maturation never occur. The core family, moreover, offers few if any traits that conform to the normal fictional model.

To begin with, the unstable family, although changing, maintains its dubious contours, replacing a strumpet mother (Elsa) with a career-woman mother (Anne). It manifests none of the family's "typical" qualities: the comfort of the hearth, the protection of home, the joys of shared meals and duties. Sagan's family—with the exception of the second mother figure Anne—prefers to these domestic attractions drinking, lovemaking, and a multidimensionally nomadic existence.

The usual power dynamic within the family has also gone awry. The father, Raymond, lacks all moral authority and wisdom. His major attributes are his looks and his sexual energy. Metaphorical hints of satyriasis:—he is a "faun,"[8] a "buck goat" (*BT,* 39)—indicate the only kind of action that interests him. Superficial, a bon vivant, a "Peter Pan" personality, refusing all responsibility, Raymond echoes his daughter's adolescent longings rather than articulating a way to adulthood. When, for example, the two of them realize that Anne has left them for good, they both sit down "like schoolchildren" (*BT,* 179) to write letters of apology to her.

Anne, on the other hand, rejects passivity, the tried and true mode of the mother figure. She inhabits her authority naturally and even in a rare tender moment with Cécile never loses her iron grip. Her personality is represented metonymically by her powerful car that she drives as a man would: she has no need of a dominant male. On their outing to Saint Raphael, with Raymond and Cécile next to her, for example, she steers the car through the mountain passes "symbolizing the family they will become" (*BT,* 142). Anne, then, heads the fledgling family, governing both the father-child and the daughter-child. However, despite the several indications of her penchant for squelching their gestures of independence,[9] she is also more principled and more vulnerable than her ersatz charges.

Cécile, the child, the strongest willed of all, combats the "bourgeois novel" (*BT,* 110)—the happy extended family—taking shape without her consent. She understands her new position of "daughter" as a role thrust upon her that must be played out, a role that does not correspond to any profound need or desire. At seventeen, she drinks too much, loves fast cars, and resembles more a skinny cat than a ripening woman. Her amorality hardly disturbs her. She has, then, nothing in common with such dutiful daughters as Louisa May Alcott's *Little Women*, Carolyn Keene's Nancy Drew, or the Countess de Ségur's *Les petites filles modèles* (Exemplary little girls). In fact, while primarily an observer in the first third of the novel, in the last part she directs and organizes all the crises. She needs no guidance from the adult world in order to operate successfully.

We might try to interpret, in a Bettelheimian sense,[10] this family romance as a type of Snow White or Sleeping Beauty fairy story, an interpretation encouraged by the novel's allusions to such tales. The many leitmotivs, among others the sea and the pine forest as sites of sexual initiation, reinforce the novel's fablelike quality. In this light, Cécile (princess/young girl) destroys Anne (evil stepmother/displaced figure of primary bonding) in order to claim and realize her own sexuality. Anne, indeed, thwarts Cécile's affair with Cyril on several occasions and thereby precipitates Cécile's headlong rush into sexual experience. *Bonjour Tristesse* could, then, be considered an initiation rite—with the protagonist taking leave of her parents and preparing to enter into a "normal" adult relationship.

This interpretation, however, is fraught with problems. Cyril, for example, if handsome and strong, stable, committed, and trustworthy, does not have the requisite charisma. Cécile does not want a prince who is as bourgeois as her evil stepmother. When Anne dies, Cyril "dies" with her. Cécile, it seems, wants no other prince than her father. If she rids herself of Anne, it is to preserve her special rapport with daddy. She clearly adores him, speaking of their dancing together, for instance, as though they were lovers (*BT,* 54).

Nevertheless, a reading of the novel as simply an incest fantasy overlooks a more important and dominant liaison between Cécile and Raymond. As indicated, the father and daughter, replicas of each other, dwell in an appealing psychological paradise of freedom and irresponsibility. This is the complicity that Cécile intends to defend—the borders of their insouciance.

Insouciance must not be understood here as infantilism. We might even, as Janice Radway does, comprehend the polar opposite and conventional ending of a Harlequin romance as a much more common fantasy of continued childhood dependence.[11] In Radway's interpretation, the sexual initiation and marriage that cap a Harlequin romance represent, ultimately, not a sexual maturation but a fantasy of total regression to the protection of the all-satisfying "mother"—become the character of the husband in the novel. Cécile, indeed, is tempted several times to seek this kind of dependence on Cyril and, moreover, especially on Anne. However, in the end, what Cécile demands and achieves is a kind of "being-in-solitude," a solitude only partially mitigated by the presence of her father, whom she, after all, controls.

Thus we can read the killing off or getting rid of Anne as a necessary action to arrive at a certain awareness of absence, and, as a consequence, a coming to grips with one's solitude. This contrasts markedly with the conquering of a triumphant wholeness, predicated as the happy ending of the standard family romance. Sagan introduces this desired state of aloneness or alterity, inscribed within a consciousness of absence, from the very beginning of *Bonjour Tristesse* and in all the elements of the "pre-text": the title and the excerpt of Eluard's poem that prefaces the story. [12]

In Eluard's poem, "sadness"—the sadness the narrator welcomes at the novel's end after Anne has died—signifies the presence in phantasmatic form of the loved one. Eluard's poem evokes a state of being in which nonbeing is palpable; the absent one is a shadow enrobed in the emotions of the lover. The perception of the other through memory makes possible both a private fullness and a piercing knowledge of lack or emptiness.

Cécile evolves, within the narrative, in the fullness of this lack, this absence. More important, by consciously separating herself from Anne, the mother figure, she orchestrates this evolution on her own, assuming the responsibility for her solitude and her emptiness. We can think of *Bonjour Tristesse,* therefore, as a radical reworking of the family romance model and an unorthodox victory for the protagonist.

Nevertheless, the reader can only experience Cécile's victory ambiguously. First of all, in terms of the story line, Cécile realizes her goals by destroying a mostly admirable character. Second, Sagan's narrative strategies—the two most noteworthy of which include her preoccupation with tone and her voicing technique—complicate the reader's reception of the text and rapport with the central character.

The bittersweet and melancholic tone conveyed through the Eluard poem that serves as epigraph appears again immediately in the first paragraph of the novel, and, indeed, braces the entire text. From the beginning, the first-person narrator meditates on her present emotional state, a sadness that, like a "silk cocoon" (*BT,* 13), has enveloped her, separating her from others. This silk ("soie" in French—by homophonic analogy "soi" or self) that now possesses her, also permits her a language by which she can speak her solitude and, therefore, recount the disturbing adventure that led to her current heavyhearted state.

Sagan intermittently reinforces the feeling of impending tragedy imparted by the tone of the first pages in images such as that of the "ravishing seashell" (*BT,* 42), a former good luck charm found on the ocean floor, which causes the narrator now holding it in her hand to weep. Despite moments of sensuousness, satire, and even burlesque, the tone remains predominantly one of tearful nostalgia. This overall atmospheric stasis counters the notion that Cécile has won a victory in claiming her independent self.

What really troubles the reader in regards to Cécile's quest, however, (and what may be the most intriguing aspect of *Bonjour Tristesse*) is the reader's relationship to the narrator-protagonist Cécile. All that can be known or understood about the characters and the situation is filtered through Cécile's mind. From the outset, the reader shares her perspective and point of view. Sagan facilitates this identification by presenting at first a sensitive, agreeably precocious, and humorously self-conscious narrator: "I stretched out in the sand, took a handful of it and let the grains slide through my fingers in a soft yellow stream; I thought to myself that it was slipping away just like time, that that was a banal idea, and that it was quite fine to indulge in such hackneyed thoughts" (*BT,* 15–16).

Yet, while both the lucidity of this first-person narrator and her harmless hedonism prompt a ready identification, the narrator-protagonist eventually demonstrates something of the "bad seed" personality. In the last chapter, for example, while shamefacedly admitting her responsibility for Anne's disappearance, Cécile lights up a cigarette at the dinner table—a gesture Anne would never have permitted. She obviously takes great pleasure in this retrospective and spiteful act of revolt.

Both attractive and hateful, more Gidean than Dickensian, Sagan's first-person narrator frequently repulses the readers by her hypocrisy, then reels them back in by her evocation of the bliss of young love or by anticipating their own objections to her actions: "I thought about [my revenge on Anne] so hard that I sat down on my bed, my heart pounding, and said to myself that it was all stupid and grotesque, that I was just a spoiled and lazy kid, and that I didn't have the right to think that way" (*BT*, 76). The narrator's remarkable insights into her own psyche encourage the reader to think of her as an especially bright and, in the end, normal adolescent, but her insidious plotting against Anne establishes her as a kind of monster.

Moreover, in *Bonjour Tristesse,* the first-person narrator perturbs the reader not merely in one time dimension, but in two, for the narrating "I" is really two I's, which we might call the "Future" or "Experienced" I and the "Present" or "Acting" I. Both I's possess the powers of introspection, thus the Experienced I can reflect upon herself at the moment of telling the story just as the Acting I reflects upon herself as she acts. The Experienced (and older) I, closer to the reader in time, births the narrative of her past out of her present emotional state, meditates upon that state, and, also, comments on the Acting (or younger) I, who participates in the story being told. In the following passage, for example, the Experienced I intelligently analyzes the self-indulgent attitude of the Acting I: "[Acting I] That notion of quick, violent, and fugitive love affairs seduced me. [Experienced I] I wasn't old enough for the seductions of faithfulness" (*BT*, 21).

Although capable of examining the younger self, the Experienced I is not a reformed version of a prior self. She, too, accepts that the only coherent aspect of her personality is a taste for pleasure (*BT*, 32). The narration, in fact, frequently passes from one time frame to the other without a noticeable difference in perception or a major change in attitude. In most instances, the two frames remain indistinct.

The real and crucial difference, however, is the sadness that permeates the Experienced I's comments, and the fact that this Experienced I englobes and weights the narration. This older I, then, whom we might also label the "Other," the emergent self probed at the beginning of the novel, makes tangible to the reader an aura of melancholy, rendering it more commanding than the ups and downs of the story being told. Hypnotic as this aspect of the narrative voice is, however, it cannot annul the disquieting and ultimately homicidal narcissism of the younger I. A reader, then, might well end up disturbed by his or her own inability to choose between condemning or pitying Cécile, while taking pleasure in the sweet sadness that pervades the narration.

Whatever way in which the reader receives the text, the family romance as depicted in *Bonjour Tristesse* shocks. Sagan's novel refutes the pattern of the girl's eventual acceptance of her role as "woman" and her consequent reinsertion into a new patriarchal family. Furthermore, the novel's treatment of Cécile, who gets what she wants in the end, imposes this state of self-conscious solitude as desirable.

Un certain sourire

Dominique Gets What She Earns. Dominique and her titular boyfriend Bertrand, both law students at the Sorbonne, end their afternoon of listening to a café's juke box and discussing literature by having a drink with Bertrand's uncle Luc, an international businessman. When Luc invites them to lunch later that week "with his wife," Dominique realizes she would rather have discovered that he was single. Up to this point, her life has seemed uneventful, marked principally by an apathy that has allowed her to drift with the tide, most recently gravitating to the pull of Bertrand's possessive love. Luc, however, stirs up something that eclipses the habitual boredom shadowing her existence.

As soon as Luc's wife Françoise leaves Paris for a vacation in the country, Luc begins to pursue Dominique. She cannot, however, quite grasp his intentions, because, while escorting her to a variety of night clubs and restaurants, he limits his sexual overtures to one off-hand proposition of a brief affair. The prospect of a fling with Luc, even if dangerous, excites Dominique. It frees her to engage in a series of risky ventures, including a petting session in a movie theater with a completely unknown boy.

At the start of the weekend after Françoise's return, when the older and younger couples leave for an overnight visit to Bertrand's mother's country estate, Dominique's exuberance grinds to a halt. Life redefines itself as a gaggle of rules and Françoise proves again to be too kind to allow Dominique to discount her feelings. How could she think of betraying her? Luc, on the other hand, brazenly embraces Dominique in the estate's labyrinthine garden and soon she can think of nothing else.

She lives out her surrender to his latest appeal: "Afterwards I'll go back to Françoise, What do you risk?,"[13] by displacing her desire onto a final crazy night of be-bop and booze (and what they lead to) with Bertrand. At the end of her exams, Dominique acknowledges that the school year is "finally over" (*UCS, 32*), implying that the sensual lesson is the most meaningful one she has learned: if Luc summons her for a tryst during vacation, she will answer the call.

After two hazy months at home in the Yonne with distant and preoccupied parents, Dominique meets up with Luc in Avignon from where they drive to the sea for a fifteen-day idyll. There, she discovers the satisfaction of romantic symbiosis. For Dominique, this means no more role-playing, no more absence from herself, but also no weakness in succumbing to the temptation of an all-encompassing love. She does surrender, however, and loses herself in Luc. She even plunges into the depths of his exalted sadness, joining him in his withdrawal from the world.

Upon returning to Paris, to the new school year, and to the status quo of Luc's marriage, Dominique realizes that she has indeed fallen in love. She suffers. She suffers when Bertrand poses the ultimatum "him or me," and she chooses, without much hope of reciprocity, Luc. She suffers when her loquacious friend Catherine tries to cheer her up with some well-meaning popular psychology. She suffers but finds some solace when fellow student Alain analyzes her passion as though it were a novel. The most wretched patch occurs when Luc breaks off their affair completely because Françoise has discovered the truth about them. To make matters worse, Dominique is unable to stop herself from confessing her love and pain to him.

Luc's business takes him to America for several weeks and, in the vacuum this creates, Dominique submerges herself in her unhappiness. Although he regrets hurting her, Luc makes his position clear by not calling her for fifteen days after his return. When he does, she agrees to meet, having meanwhile understood and accepted that she is really alone again. She cannot keep herself from smiling over this new knowledge.

Reading the Family Romance in *Un certain sourire*.   Sagan's second novel, less accomplished than her first, again would seem to treat the initiation of a young girl into womanhood by means of her discovery of sexuality. In fact, as in *Bonjour Tristesse,* the protagonist's critical recognition is of her aloneness, her separateness, and, thus, her "self"—not a socially constructed or psychologically determined woman, but a being-in-solitude. The love affair in *Un certain sourire* does not mask the family romance as in the earlier novel: in *Bonjour Tristesse* the parallel love stories of Cécile and Cyril, Anne and Raymond obscure, particularly in the first part of the novel, Sagan's central concern with Cécile as agent of self-awareness. Rather, in the second novel the heroine's love affair coincides exactly with her growing sense of identity. Dominique's lover Luc is also the displaced father. She finds her "self" by losing herself in him. In *Un certain sourire,* Sagan, then, devotes more time to the sexual initiation which consequently becomes an ironic and extended trope for selfhood.

In noting that *Un certain sourire* pales in comparison to *Bonjour Tristesse,* we do not mean that Sagan eliminates or modifies her bittersweet tone, so important in communicating the feeling of solitariness. As in *Bonjour Tristesse,* in *Un certain sourire,* a mood of melancholia, harboring cautious emotional changes within, is prominent from the beginning paragraphs of the novel to its end. Sagan reinforces this mood through poignant images of Paris as seen by Dominique at dusk or in the early morning, such as this view of the river: "The sky was white over a Seine seated between its metal cranes like a sad child surrounded by its toys" (*UCS,* 39).

However, in *Un certain sourire,* Sagan does not employ the voicing strategy predominant in *Bonjour Tristesse*——that is, a dimension of the "I" who looks back with regret on the recounted adventure. The narrative voicing on the whole holds neither the fascination nor the ambiguity of the complex first-person narrator of the former novel. The "I" of *Un certain sourire* is only the Acting I telling the story in the past. There is no additional distancing of a second "I" who reflects upon herself at the time of the telling as well as upon the Acting I. Furthermore, the "I," or Dominique, has less energy, less wit, and fewer conflicts to face than the multifaceted Cécile of *Bonjour Tristesse.* No worthy rival blocks Dominique's path to self-indulgence. No surfeit of narratable lucidity keeps engaging the reader's sympathy immediately after he or she has been repulsed by an overdose of bad faith.

The family romance takes on, however, some interesting contours in *Un certain sourire.* The displacement of emotional attachment again shows how Sagan reimagines in perverse terms the oedipal drama, while the novel's outcome complements what we have already seen posited by Sagan as the unorthodox but desired state of an emergent woman's being-in-the-world. Once again, the "family" proves an odd triangular configuration with the pivotal figure, the "daughter" Dominique, a teenaged narrator orphaned in Paris. Her biological parents, remote, uninvolved, and deadened by their mourning over a son long-since passed away, remain insignificant specters. Nearly absent from the narrative, they appear twice, mentioned only in passing by Dominique in the two instances when she returns home. The first of these sojourns (part 2, chapter 2) functions primarily as a psychological regression. Seduced by the smells and sounds of her childhood, Dominique becomes a little girl again. This allows her to give in to the demands of the father substitute Luc.

At the beginning of the story, Dominique, unstructured and floating, wanders through the motions of young womanhood, including an

appropriate romance with the serious Bertrand and law courses in
Paris. Neither romance nor studies gives her a sense of self-definition.
She sees herself, instead, as playing out a series of roles. Throughout
the novel, the great barrier to her happiness, until her affair with Luc,
will be her ability to stand apart and watch herself perform an expected
role. She counters this with internal battles against performance. She
therefore bounces back and forth from states of melancholic inertia to
excessive freedom, as in the encounter in the movie theater where she
allows a total stranger to fondle her.

Luc, not unlike Raymond of *Bonjour Tristesse,* resembles his "daughter." He sees himself in Dominique: "we are the same character" (*UCS,*
38), just as she recognizes herself immediately in him, in his face with
its features "a thousand times [more familiar] than Bertrand's" (*UCS,*
26). Whereas Raymond and Cécile share an addiction to irresponsibility and frivolousness, Luc and Dominique share an inability to be
happy, to find a niche in which to ignore the anguish of their aloneness.

Luc, nevertheless, initiates Dominique in certain survival skills, in-
troducing her to the sea, a metaphor for passion; to money, a form of
power; to driving, one of Sagan's consistent literary projections of vital
energy. His attentions, his respect, and his desire allow her, she feels,
to conceive of herself as deserving of respect and desire. Dominique
sees herself positively through him. And as he is her double, he gives
her a stronger sense of her own self, magnified not as the other, but as
the same. When the inevitable breakup occurs, foreseen in the first
paragraph of the novel by the song "Lone and Sweet," the selection on
the juke box, Dominique can reclaim her solitude. If wounded by Luc,
she has also learned from him how to choose her fate. Solitude is not
inflicted upon her.

Dominique's similarity to the father figure Luc, their echoing sadness, is understood by the mother figure Françoise as "destined to be
consoled by Venus types, like me" (*UCS,* 141). A softened, sweetened,
and passive version of Anne of *Bonjour Tristesse,* an earth mother—
round, blond, and generous—Françoise explicitly wishes that Dominique were her daughter. She buys her clothes, nourishes her body and
her mind by providing a haven during exams, and even attempts to
comfort her after the debacle of her affair with Luc. Dominique accepts
all this of her, seeking out Françoise, the very person she has wronged,
as the only one capable of helping her survive her suffering. Dominique
can at first ignore Françoise's feelings because she appears both completely malleable and completely resistant to hurt. Later, Françoise's

undemanding selflessness appears to Dominique as an example of the horrors of the world. In *Un certain sourire,* then, the mother figure Françoise, like Anne in *Bonjour Tristesse,* again provides a negative model. She also goes unrewarded, except in martyrdom, for her pains. Dominique, on the contrary, reaps the benefits of her nonconformity. By conjoining with the uncle of her lover, a paternal replacement, her masculine double, she begins the process that will assure her self-possession. While Luc refuses to give up the security of the nurturing Françoise, Dominique accepts finally, through parthenogenesis, the birthing of her self-in-solitude.

The process of refusing and then accepting this solitary self is figured throughout the novel in episodes of nausea. In part 1, chapter 8, after her last evening of lovemaking with Bertrand, Dominique recognizes the gap between her imagined essential self and the self that acts. She becomes ill and stays ill for over a week. Her illness—in fact, a sign of her emptiness or lack of fullness—paradoxically represented as a pregnancy scare, can only be cured by Luc. Their liaison will allow her momentarily to feel whole. The second episode of nausea occurs in Cannes (part 2, chapter 2) during their vacation. Dominique, exhausted after many sleepless nights, suddenly recognizes the fragility of her love affair. She breaks out in a sweat, feels as though a fog were closing in on her, and comes close to death. This attack of panic gives form to her anguish at the apprehension of her fundamental aloneness. The third episode takes place when Dominique, in bed again with Luc, props herself up to kiss him (part 3, chapter 3). Nausea overwhelms her, signifying her understanding of his emotional absence and, again, her aloneness.

While any knowledge of contemporary French letters makes the connection between these attacks and the prototypical existential crisis entertainingly overt, Sagan, unlike Sartre, does not cure Dominique's urge to vomit by large doses of social commitment. Besides, Dominique's problem is not the generalized human one—"Who am I?" "Why do I exist?"—but the more specific female one: "Do I exist without a/my man?" Dominique's difficulty in coming to grips with a separate existence keeps on upsetting her until the last third of the novel.

Having created a nontraditional "woman-in-the-works" attempting to hold out against social conditioning, Sagan finally resorts to the traditional medicine to make Dominique well—time. To signal Dominique's arrival at health and at a sense of self, Sagan effects a medical metamorphosis of her images—the emptiness becoming overfullness,

the absence manifesting itself as too much presence. Thus in the last
and distanced episode of nausea (part 3, chapter 4), Dominique *remembers* a bout of illness when she kissed Luc for the first time in Cannes.
What she recalls is not her solitude and Luc's absence from her but
rather how the absence that had always marked her own life disappeared with Luc's presence. Yet this presence also causes her to feel sick
to her stomach. For the first time, she thinks of Luc as suffocating
her. Her nausea here results from overstuffing rather than under-
nourishment.

When she has at last come to terms with her aloneness and Luc
phones after returning from his long trip to America, Dominique senses that something oozes out of her ("s'écoulait") and escapes ("s'enfuy-
ait" [*UCS,* 188]), bringing her relief from an obsessive and sickening
phantom. The smile that forms on her lips, despite herself, heralds her
liberation, just as the music that accompanies her down the stairs, a
lively moment of Mozart, bespeaks a kind of happiness. Although she
partakes at the end of the novel of the bittersweet emotional coloration
present from the beginning, now the mood claims her as a true initiate.
A sort of pleasure predicated on absence, violently intuited by the narrator in the first paragraph of *Un certain sourire,* envelops the novel's
ending.

What Do Girls Want?

Our readings of Sagan's first two novels have shown how she de-
legitimates the family romance plot and consequently calls into question the premises on which the family romance rests: loving the "father" does not necessarily mean prolonging patriarchy. Sagan's
heroines, while indeed awakening to sexual desire, neither marry nor,
as the other standard alternative, go mad at the end of her novels.[14]
Bonjour Tristesse and *Un certain sourire* transcend any oversimplified oedipal drama.

As we have seen, Sagan inverts or transforms the givens of the family
romance by strategies of reparenting (changing the conventional patriarchal model) or regendering (ascribing psychological or physical
characteristics to one sex that have been typically attributed to the
other). A substitute family replaces the biological one, making possible
not just the projection but also, as in *Un certain sourire,* the fulfillment
of desire through the surrogate.

Nevertheless, satisfaction of desire does not guarantee the passage into scrupulous womanhood or into the social structure. Nor does the heroine become capable of transferring her desire for the father figure onto a nonfamily member closer to her own age. In fact, the converse occurs: a love affair with a boy leads to a return of desire for the original father (Raymond in *Bonjour Tristesse*) or to a new father figure (Luc in *Un certain sourire*). The oedipal complex would, then, appear to be reinforced rather than resolved.

We might call these implications of incest, even in their convoluted forms, clever means of subverting the sex-gender system. By keeping the romance within the family, Sagan evacuates the larger social structure. In later texts, most notably the Van Milhem pieces *(Château en Suède, Des bleus à l'âme),* such a subversive intent appears much more obvious as the incest constellation involves a brother and sister who, by loving each other and taking refuge in an endless adolescence, avoid altogether the family romance and its implications for the continuation of a society based on the exchange of women.

Moreover, the fathers' and daughters' similarities discourage any notion of a hierarchical social system constructed by gender or age. In both early novels, the father figure, rather than representing stability and order, conveys fecklessness and disarray. As irresponsible and disconnected as the daughter figure/protagonist, the father is in no position to teach her acceptance of a social role. The "fathers" Raymond and Luc have never accepted such roles themselves.

The mother figures, whether masculinized and assertive (Anne in *Bonjour Tristesse*) or overfeminized and accommodating (Françoise in *Un certain sourire*), do not present any more positive guides than the fathers. Neither position—daring to be independent or offering up oneself to everybody's needs—when couched within the terms of the couple, ballasts the mother figure's self-worth or sexual confidence. In this regard Anne's death would seem directly tied to her sexual repression, which we glean through her inability to accept the sexual pull of the pine forest, an aversion that terminates in her feverish flight from it. She is, then, as damned by her aggressive "masculine" refusal as is Françoise—one of the few characters in Sagan's fiction who cooks—by her long-suffering "feminine" acquiescence.

Given these pessimistic characterizations of grown men and women, it is quite revealing that Sagan chooses to establish androgynous adolescent heroines. Both Cécile *(Bonjour Tristesse)* and Dominique *(Un certain sourire),* although clearly attracted to males, are physically underdeveloped, boyish in fact. They like, in a stereotypical masculine way, to drink and drive fast. Both also, very aware of required social role-playing, prefer to control or create their own roles. As a result they are the most virile (if we understand virile as vigorous, forceful, and capable of [pro]creating) of the two novels' characters, relying on no one but themselves to establish the rules. They, also, but especially Cécile, tend to see men as objects of consumption, therefore adopting a prevalent male attitude toward the opposite sex.

Scrappers, each one defeats in a gutsy battle her enemy—in Cécile's case, Anne; in Dominique's, the presence of Luc within her. Again, in taking into consideration the prescriptions of the family romance, we note that these personalities and the protagonists' resulting skirmishes allay the possibility of arriving at the "acceptable" happy ending. But if androgyny fosters the "daughters'" permanent alienation, it also permits Cécile and Dominique to arrive at a form of psychic haven, sheltered from the codes of subservience and obeisance.

In *Bonjour Tristesse* and *Un certain sourire*, Sagan sabotages conventional notions about what girls want and conventional narrative solutions to girls' fate. She also problematizes the family structure by laying bare certain dangers of role acceptance as well as dangers of role refusal. We do not suggest, however, that she proposes an alternative to the standard model. For all her scrambling of the family romance, she certainly does not intend to provide an example of radical feminine behavior.

Self-involved and destructive of others, neither Cécile nor Dominique can be considered exemplary. Nonetheless, because of the seductive nature of the confessional first-person narration, both draw the reader in closer than do any of Sagan's later fictional protagonists in either her other first-person or more numerous third-person texts.[15] The doubled voice of Cécile, especially, catches up the reader in the character's vitality and charismatic quickness. But, as commented upon earlier, the complex voicing technique of this first novel also destabilizes reader identification, promoting a parodoxical if tantalizing rapport with the protagonist, a feat that Sagan never quite matches in any of her later novels. This complex voice may well be Sagan's most effective tactic for getting the reader to ask difficult questions about identity formation and the psychosocial structuring of "woman."

What she also achieves in both *Bonjour Tristesse* and *Un certain sourire* and maintains with few exceptions throughout her mostly pithy and classically structured corpus is a mood that conveys how the protagonist experiences life. The wide-eyed wonder, dewy-eyed innocence, or proudly won insightfulness of the heroine of the conventional romance gives way to an enticing bittersweetness. This is the tone that bodies forth both Cécile's and Dominique's awareness of their solitude.

Despite many thematic correspondences to women's romances and, more specifically in her early novels, to the family romance plot, Sagan's texts, unlike such ending-oriented narratives, draw their strength in great part from the orchestration of this haunting melancholic tone. In this, she may well approach the "emotional realism" of which Raymond Williams speaks when he discusses readers' enjoyment of novels that assure them that life's emotions are always being stirred up and happiness is, after all, a precarious business. [16]

Chapter Three

The Mixed Message of Sagan's Third-Person Love Stories

Make Love, Make War

Françoise Sagan's love stories might better be termed war stories. The author herself contends: "Love is war—a battle in which one person tries to take over the other. It's made up of jealousy, possession, and self interest, which permeate even the most generous attitudes."[1] Contrary to most romance warriors, Sagan's characters fight not merely to win, but especially to keep the combat alive. In her novels, particularly her third-person romances, love lasts as long as a titillating insecurity reigns.

As seen in her two earliest romances, Sagan's love jousts are never as simple as a one-to-one confrontation. Even as a very young writer, Sagan articulated her desire to transfer to fiction her belief that life is a "rhythmic progression of three characters."[2] Thus, the triangular, or three-party struggle, underpins all of her love plots, including the four to be examined in this chapter. Each of the different triangular configurations contributes its particular ammunition to the assault on the fragile focal couple. In *Aimez-vous Brahms . . .* (1959), as in *La Chamade* (1965), two tightly drawn and melancholic novels of the "minor mode" group, the couple disintegrates when the female character decides to return to her former lover. In *Un peu de soleil dans l'eau froide* (1969), an original and troubling variation of the triangle, the female character chooses death as the partner she prefers to her flesh and blood lover. *Le Lit défait* (1977), a "major mode" novel, jauntier and more rambling than the first three and another inventive reformulation of the triangle, pits two characters against the myth of one of them. The mythic self—a kind of Gallic "Spiderwoman"—secures only a mitigated victory in the end.

As these brief synopses suggest, the novels' resolutions, as well as the sometimes unexpected twists and turns of the triangular plots, permit a reading that divulges the dilemma in the lovers', notably the female lover's, condition. At the same time Sagan's third-person love stories afford considerable pleasure by their momentarily sustained fantasy of "the real thing."

Key Aspects of Sagan's Love Dynamics

To introduce Sagan's fictional love universe, we turn first to the way in which she develops her plots. The pattern is remarkably similar in almost all of her romances, both first- and third-person. Sagan's love stories usually begin with character A, even if involved in some kind of a relationship with character B, feeling alone and vaguely dissatisfied. Character A meets character C, who often falls head over heels in love with A. A comes to desire C as well. They make love, hiding their affair from B. Finally, they tell B, thus eliminating him (or her) from the dynamic. (This is the end of the first part, generally the first half of the novel.) A and C live out a blissful period of perfect happiness. They are completely engrossed in one another. (This is the end of the second part, frequently only a few chapters.)

"Real life" intrudes in the form of the outside world, sometimes taking the shape of character D. This precipitates a crisis. A and C begin to grow apart. More and more evidence of their separateness and the inevitable collapse of their affair accumulates. B reenters the picture. A and C break up. A is left alone, even if nominally reunited with B. (This is the end of the third part, almost as long as the first part.)

While each of the novels basic to the analysis in this chapter conforms, in general, to the model, there are several interesting divergencies. For example, in *Aimez-vous Brahms . . . ,* Character A (Paule) never bonds with character C (Simon), but remains psychologically dependent on B (Roger). In *Un peu de soleil dans l'eau froide,* character C (Nathalie), precisely because of her passionate attachment to him, leaves character A (Gilles) for the unnamed contender for whom Gilles has been standing in all along: death wins Nathalie. Gilles is left to confront his solitude without the solace of character B—his ex-mistress Eloïse. In *Le Lit défait,* character A (Béatrice) and character C (Edouard) are together from the beginning of the novel. They remain together at the end. However, Edouard's rival, character B, keeps intruding into the story and is the sum of all of Béatrice's past lovers and lovers to come. And Béatrice, to keep Edouard's love, must transform herself into another version of A by the novel's end. Therefore, in this latter novel, the suspense, which is usually encapsulated in Sagan's romances by the questions, Will A and C get together? Will they stay together?, is better represented by the apparently paradoxical query: Will A ever really love C?, Will C be able to love an A who loves him?

Although the particular ramifications of these variations will be analyzed later, it is worth noting here that Sagan relegates the idyllic phase of love to the midsection rather than to the end of her novel. That is, she never suggests a "happily-ever-after" mode. Furthermore, this perfect love lasts but a fragment of the novel's duration. By her plotting, Sagan seems to indicate that love is just a temporary hiatus between the more crushing reality of getting into and out of it.

As mentioned at the outset of this chapter, in Sagan's novels love means war, often figured as a series of power plays. Sagan almost never imagines love in terms other than pugilistic. Her love portraits are fraught with tension and danger. Gilles, in *Un peu de soleil dans l'eau froide,* remembers all of his affairs as "sad and dulled combats, occasionally lightened by moments of happiness, but always ending in victories which taste of defeat or by defeat itself.[3] Edouard, in *Le Lit défait*—the book's title suggesting not only an unmade bed but also defeat on the bedroom battlefield—denies the possibility of assimilating the two terms "lovers" and "equals."[4] Lucile in *La Chamade* tries to outmaneuver her lover Antoine in determining what will happen in their couple. And Paule, in *Aimez-vous Brahms . . . ,* if no match for the sharpshooter Roger, discovers she is almost as good at sabotaging Simon's happiness as Roger is at attacking hers. The characters' thoughts about themselves and each other image a world in which the master love strategist rivals the ace bomber pilot of World War II. Indeed, the lover possesses greater potential for destruction than the aviator does.

On the other hand, Sagan sprinkles her romances with moments of erotic unicity in which one lover can barely distinguish himself or herself from the other. Common occurrences of this special oneness include passionate reunions after separations, magnetic attractions across crowded and smoky rooms, and a supernatural sense of isolation. Simon enters this otherworldly atmosphere with Paule in *Aimez-vous Brahms . . .* when they run to meet each other outside her shop: "The gray sidewalks, the passers-by, the surrounding cars all of a sudden seemed to him like a stylized decor, rigidified and timeless. They looked at each other at a distance of two meters and before she could be lulled back to sleep by the noise and somber reality of the street, while she stood there still on tenterhooks, alert, at the extremity of her own awareness, Simon moved forward and took her in his arms."[5] For a few precious seconds, Paule and Simon comprise the only reality of their world. They are united, a group of one in the midst of an army of onlookers.

There exist, then, two basic silhouettes of love in Sagan's third-person romances: one in which each lover struggles for control over the other. Another, and contradictory one, is that in which the lovers willingly bond in such a way that they are no longer distinguishable one from the other. These silhouettes, however, are far from mutually exclusive. For example, Edouard in *Le Lit défait* develops a subtle behavioral pattern that entraps his lover Béatrice into doing exactly what he wishes. At the same time he maintains and believes that he does not exist until swept away in her orbit.

Sex, as might be expected, provides the supreme interlude for the lovers' perfect joining. Couples disappear into each other. They hear only one breath. Their hearts beat with the same rhythm. The narrator of *La Chamade* (a term that denotes the drum roll of military defeat) describes the first afternoon of incendiary lovemaking between Lucile and Antoine: "What happened to them is what always happens to a man and woman when a shared passion takes hold. Very soon, they no longer remembered experiencing pleasure with anyone else, they forgot the limits of their own bodies, modesty and audacity became confused in the same abstraction. The thought that they had to leave each other in an hour or two seemed to them despicably immoral."[6] In the act of love, Lucile and Antoine claim their couple as their only homeland and abolish any timepiece other than their own heartbeat.

This kind of love evolves for most of Sagan's characters into a veritable sickness, an addiction in which the other is necessary to prove one's own existence or, at the least, to protect one from the incursions of a harsh reality. Paule, for example, in *Aimez-vous Brahms . . .* cannot recognize herself when she looks into a mirror. She needs to see herself through her absent lover Roger's eyes. The narrator in *Le Lit défait* likens Edouard's dependence on Béatrice to a cancer victim's need for morphine. All the female characters want to be and are possessed by their men.

The most extreme and shattering description of this malady occurs not in her third-person romances but in Sagan's 1978 play *Il fait beau jour et nuit* (It's beautiful night and day). An exalted Zelda, the main character, speaks of her passion:

> You can't imagine the debauchery, the words, the cries and whispers unleashed by the absence of any witness. I order a man to listen, to touch, to look at no one but me, and I only listen, look, embrace him. He is submerged, invaded, overwhelmed by me. I tell him everything; I tell him to hurt me, and, at certain moments, I tell him I was first in history at school. I tell him that I'll kill him if he cheats on me, but I tell him that I'm afraid of lightning. And he tells me everything, too, everything which goes through his mind at that very instant—and especially when the rush of blood ebbs after our lovemaking. At a given moment, I know that he has accepted me, he sees me, he wants me, he wants me to live. It is necessary and indispensable to somebody that I live, that I be me, Zelda, that he see me, silent and naked, with his own eyes. Then, I can breathe.[7]

In Zelda's monologue, we see that she creates a self in terms of her lover, and that even this self, once created, becomes silent and completely exposed to her lover's eyes. His gaze permits her to breathe.

The latent masochism suggested in Zelda's surrender to an other is reinforced constantly as a major trait of nearly half of the characters in the novels under discussion. Paule and Simon in *Aimez-vous Brahms . . .*, Nathalie in *Un peu de soleil dans l'eau froide,* Edouard in *Le Lit défait,* and even Lucile and Antoine in *La Chamade,* though to a lesser degree, want to be hurt. They want, especially, never to settle into loving and being loved. Even if they do not, as Paule does not, consciously enjoy being wounded, their behavior encourages their lovers to assault them emotionally. This desire to live with "une écharde," a splinter (*C,* 180), always pricking the otherwise smooth surface of the love affair, undercuts or complicates the lovers' moments of complete thralldom.

Sagan's characters make war, then, not only on each other but also on their own capacities to love. To thrive, love needs the ongoing trauma of insecurity as well as the security of oneness. This dichotomous profile suggests an impossible emotional state, a self-contradictory absolutism that can only exist as fantasy.

Indeed, Sagan encases her love stories in a spatiotemporal frame that removes them from the everyday and gives them a barely concealed fairy-tale aspect. Three of the four novels in question begin in the springtime, the archetypal moment of love's awakening. The lovers experience their perfect passion during the summer, when they are on vacation from "real life." Summer makes possible unending stretches of time that do not have to be counted. Nevertheless, love, like the leaves, begins to fade in the fall. In *La Chamade* and *Un peu de soleil dans l'eau froide,* the central love affair dies completely in the winter. In *Le Lit défait,* the heroine just barely learns how to keep an affair blooming as a new spring rolls around. The only novel that does not follow this particular seasonal pattern is *Aimez-vous Brahms . . .,* whose course moves from the fall to the spring. This contributes from the beginning to building pessimistic expectations about the outcome of the love affair between Paule and Simon. It also renders Paule's masochistic reconciliation with Roger all the more ironic.

Sagan creates characters who vibrate with such seasonal changes. The focal character or the narrator frequently measures emotional intensity in terms of the amount of sunlight or the kind of wind that is blowing. Except for such references to an omnipresent nature, however, Sagan's fictional universe is relatively free of material details. This, too, imparts a "once-upon-a-time" feeling.

Posed in opposition to the good earth is a mythically bad Paris. The City exerts an endless pull, almost exclusively on the male characters. It functions as Paule's chief competition for Roger (*Aimez-vous Brahms . . .*) and as a Svengali who incites the Gilles of provincial Limoges to transform himself from a feminized (e.g., sensitive) man into a crude masculinized product of a Parisian version of the American locker room (*Un peu de soleil dans l'eau froide*). Yet occasional sketches of the multichimneyed roof tops or of the diverse personalities of the bridges over the Seine also depict a Paris as dreamy as it is dangerous.

The truly idealized part of the love affair takes place, nonetheless, not in the streets of Paris, but, rather in a well-protected bed, with an occasional jaunt to the enchanted Bois de Boulogne, the forest that skirts Paris's western border. The bed is the major prop of Sagan's romances. *La Chamade, Un peu de soleil dans l'eau froide,* and *Le Lit défait* all start in bed, while the aching problem for the central character of *Aimez-vous Brahms . . .* is a bed that has been empty for too long. But beds are never simply beds: in *La Chamade,* the bed that is a "miraculous raft" (*C,* 124) at the beginning of the love affair becomes an "out-of-control ship" (*C,* 216) at the end. In *Le Lit défait,* the characters, as in the Eluard poem that inspired the title, fly away on a bed transformed into a kind of floating banner to a never-never land of glorious passion, to a space that is no space and a time that is no time. Edouard revels in the memory that "During those days and nights of [lovemaking] the landscape around [them] had not changed in the slightest: rivers of carpeting, hills of sheets, suns of sensuality" (*LD,* 24). Natural landscapes and bedscapes here bespeak, in a collapsed comparison, the free and purely sensual space of love.

The color of Béatrice's bedroom, all in light blue as is her sitting room, draws out and reinforces this geographical insistence on a fantastical love space. Blue connotes paradise for Edouard. This celestial hue tinges also the lovely apartment of Charles, Lucile's protector (*La Chamade*), and the salon in Limoges where Gilles meets Nathalie Sylvener (*Un peu de soleil dans l'eau froide*). And while this dominant and transporting color and the many seemingly winged beds and bedrooms in Sagan's novels englobe the characters in an ongoing fantasy, the car, another permanent component of Sagan's decor, unfixed in time and space because always moving, whisks her lovers away in a self-contained sexual escapade.

Thus a magical spatial frame, as well as a mythic temporal one, isolate the lovers from the other characters in Sagan's third-person romances. This particular spatiotemporal dimension helps establish a love universe unanchored in material details and everyday life. Neither spatial nor temporal frame, however, is set up in such a way as to exclude other conceptions of time and space. The secondary characters in Sagan's novels, for example, provide a link to a passage of time unbounded by the inevitable progression toward parting. The fictional world they inhabit—dinner parties, receptions, and opening nights at the theater—suggests a turbulent universe far removed from the erotic haven of the principles. Their world, like the secondary characters themselves, is less inviting, more hostile, and more cruel.

While her secondary characters tend to represent various compromises for living in the public domain, Sagan's lovers, functioning in a private one, can be grouped into two fundamental types. The possibility of typing her main characters underscores the fantasy mode already evoked in her vertiginous portraits of love and through her spatiotemporal frames, for the characters, too, partake of the fairy tale and mythic. Sagan creates first the *puer aeternus,* or eternal adolescent, common in her theater as well. This is the character who rejects responsibility, lives only in the present, expects and needs no emotional commitment to enjoy sexual relations, and characterizes himself or herself by a narcissistic insouciance: Roger (*Aimez-vous Brahms . . .*), Lucile (*La Chamade*), Gilles (*Un peu de soleil dans l'eau froide*), and Béatrice (*Le Lit défait*). Second, Sagan fashions the love addict, a type sketched earlier. The love addict has no definition without the presence of a significant other. She or he frequently lives in the past or in fear of the future. Paule and Simon (*Aimez-vous Brahms . . .*), Nathalie (*Un peu de soleil dans l'eau froide*), and Edouard (*Le Lit défait*) belong to this latter category.

On the whole, within each category, the characters remain true to type. Variations and combinations, however, do occur. Roger, if an eternal adolescent, is also a "real man." That is, he takes a vigorous interest in his work and strives to protect his woman. Charles of *La Chamade,* while clearly sick with love for Lucile, also possesses the real man's traits. He appears, furthermore, almost godlike in his acceptance of Lucile's weaknesses. His rival Antoine, glum and oversensitive in an adolescent way, also goes through stages of love addiction and real manhood. He is the least typed of Sagan's male characters but also the most unlikable. Béatrice, although carefree, is neither lost nor aimless, as are most of the adolescent types. She adores her acting career and has a Balzacian survival energy about her.

Sagan encourages the reader to see all these main characters, whether more or less strictly typed, whether or not nurturing interests other than his or her lover, in terms of the love affair. These principal players do not, then, easily resist critical relegation to a sphere of the imaginary greatly distanced from the here and now. Their complexity, when they are complex, has chiefly to do with the art of loving.

In the midst of their greatest pain, during their most awful offense to their companion, all of Sagan's lovers invariably adhere to a code of politeness and personal elegance. Even when Gilles experiences the humiliations of a nervous breakdown *(Un peu de soleil dans l'eau froide),* he tries to laugh at himself. Sagan's characters control their reactions during scenes of parting and confession. They never take advantage of the other's suffering. They always attempt to help preserve the dignity of the partner they are betraying. Their most extreme demonstration of emotion is to shiver *(grelotter).* Throughout Sagan's corpus, this omnipresent shiver connotes fear of the end of love and anxiety at the thought of separation.

Her third-person narrators share the sensitivity and the reserve of the characters. The narrator's comments are often understated and never coarse, while descriptions of sexual encounters are veiled and elliptical. Neither sentimentality nor sensationalism colors the narrator's point of view. Yet for all that, the reader grasps the characters' passion and hurt.

One of the unrelenting ways in which Sagan communicates her lovers' emotional state is in the use of the adverbs "perfectly" (*parfaitement*) and "calmly" (*tranquillement*) and the adjectives "calm" (*tranquille*), "desperate" (*désespéré*), and "empty" (*vide*). Quite frequently these terms appear in combination. Lucile, for example, is "parfaitement désespéré et parfaitement tranquille, vidée" when she believes that her affair with Antoine has reached an end (*C,* 136). Nathalie of *Un peu de soleil dans l'eau froide,* the most desperate of all the characters, speaks only "calmly" (*PS,* 72), "in a calm voice" (*PS,* 222), or "unexcitedly" (*PS,* 237). Sagan's recurrent grouping of these adjectives and adverbs from apparently contradictory semantic fields establishes a tension akin to the emotional paralysis death or hopelessness induce. It is as if, for Sagan, the lover inhabits simultaneously the space of love (which is perfection) and the horror of love's end (which is nothingness, emptiness, or calm).

Their emotional control may save Sagan's characters from making spectacles of themselves. It may also protect the readers from vicariously experiencing such scenes. However, the absence of outbursts, tears, or other forms of physical release and the incessant reminders of characters who are "perfectly calm" suggest a more profound and lingering psychological pain.

Even if we were to ascribe the employ of such expressive clusters to an unconscious writer's tic, their abundance reinforces a notion that Sagan demonstrates, in any case, in her plotting, spatiotemporal frame, and in her profile of the love affair. Love, that is, love as she depicts it, is an untenable state, founded on never-ending anxiety and existing only in the timelessness and spacelessness of fantasy. When fantasy runs out and material reality sets in, solitude takes over. And solitude not only precludes love, but also, in these third-person romances, excludes happiness.

Character after character declares that happiness only exists as a memory. Thus Paule *recalls* a moment of absolute happiness from her first marriage (*AVB,* 12). Lucile, too, *harkens back* to a time of joy (*C,* 120). And Edouard can only conceive of his current happiness as a *memory of happiness* he will enjoy in the future (*LD,* 99). For Sagan, happiness, like passion and like Baudelaire's "marvelous clouds," which contribute the epigraph and the title to Sagan's 1961 novel *Les Merveilleux Nuages,* is an illusion gliding by, somewhere, "over there . . . over there" ("là-bas . . . là-bas"). All of her third-person romances, and particularly the four under discussion here, project a fantasy space for the momentary realization of passion that in turn will become but a trace of happiness in the protagonists' and readers' mindscapes.

People mainly read Sagan's third-person romances for the love story she tells. Her authorial nods to the conventions of realism, such as the telling details of a particular Parisian milieu (Diane Mirbec's luxurious apartment in *La Chamade*), or the topical allusions (to the Vietnam War in *Un peu de soleil dans l'eau froide*), or the contemporaneity of the decor (the night clubs in *Aimez-vous Brahms . . .*), or the spirited satire of the Parisian theater and film set (*Le Lit défait*) never displace the psychology of the love affair as center of interest. Sagan has, in fact, always maintained that the real, that is, social or political reality, is not the issue of her novels, but that she hopes to create a kind of sensory truth, a special series of moments held together by a major emotion.[8] As we have seen, Sagan encloses this emotion—love—in a protected fantasy universe untouched by her satirical comments or contemporaneous details. Sometimes the lovers themselves, if belatedly, recognize the illusory nature of their romantic world.

The First Triangular Configuration: Going Home in *Aimez-vous Brahms . . .* and *La Chamade*

Six years separate the composition of *La Chamade* (1965) from *Aimez-vous Brahms . . .* (1959). Both novels are compact. Both are structured in vignettes that juxtapose dialogue with passages of description and analysis. Both have titles and informing questions referring to music. And both have plots that follow the same basic direction: the heroine leaves her lover to take a new lover; she then, after a very brief period of fulfillment (economically represented by devoting only one chapter in each novel to it), returns to the original lover.

While sustained metaphors and studied comparisons characterize neither novel, both contain a few poignant passages in which the main character experiences the environment as an extension of herself. Paule, for example, projects her own attempt to hold off aging onto a Sisyphus-like rower in the Bois de Boulogne, defying winter by his acrobatics (*AVB,* 97). Lucile anthropomorphizes the streetlamps of Paris; they, too, caught between two worlds, "always bursting into light too early, humiliated in their professional pride . . ., caught between a day which would never quite end and a dawn which was already prancing in the sky . . ." (*C,* 119).

If heroine Paule's point of view frames the earlier novel and coincides
for the most part with the narrator's position, the narrator in the later
novel, sympathetic to all members of the love triangle, takes more
distance from the characters. In fact, this narrator, whose presence is
quite obvious to the reader, comments frequently on the lovers' situation and enjoys satirizing their social milieu. *La Chamade*, then, with
a more important satirical component, is not as relentlessly introspective as *Aimez-vous Brahms . . .* in which Sagan stresses not only four
episodes of self-reflection through mirror images, but also includes one
member of the triangle as double of another. The dissection of passion
is, nevertheless, basic to both novels. And each one exposes the dangers
of "going home."

The Limits of Normalcy.   While gazing into her mirror at a
woman she only partially recognizes, Paule waits: "She had set herself
down in front of the mirror to kill time and—the thought made her
smile—she discovered that it was time that was killing her, little by
little, softly, attacking an appearance that she knew had been loved"
(*AVB*, 11–12). Paule is thirty-nine years old—a beauty growing old—
and she is tired. The object of her wait, Roger, a moderately successful
executive for his own trucking company, had early on established the
credo of their six-year liaison: sexual freedom and independence. Paule
notes ruefully to herself that he has been the only one to benefit from
this imposed liberty. She, on the other hand, has provided the shoulder
for him to cry on and the ear in which to confide his latest daredevil
adventure or romantic caprice. As a result, she has grown nearly ill
from loneliness, insecurity, and holding back her emotions.

That evening, Roger, yet again after dinner and dancing, leaves
Paule to her empty bed. Rather than assuage the sadness he detects,
he rejects Paule to take on Paris. His rationale divulges his good-na-
tured egocentrism: "He felt like listening to the sound of his own
footsteps on the paving stones, like watching over the city he knew so
well and maybe falling into an evening's adventure or two" (*AVB*, 22).

Paule's job as an interior decorator takes her to the wealthy Van den
Besh residence. She first sees the exceptionally handsome, somewhat
delicate, twenty-five-year-old son of the house, Simon, in the living
room mirror. He charms her with his enthusiastic patter. Simon, although titularly a law clerk, is, in fact, a purposeless wanderer, engaged by a celebrated lawyer doubtlessly out of deference to the
memory of a past affair with his mother, Mme Van den Besh, a volubile
ex-courtesan.

By happy coincidence, at least from Simon's perspective, he runs into Paule and Roger that evening in a night club. Simon proceeds to get drunk after informing Paule that Roger is "a real man . . . with healthy ideas" (*AVB*, 41), exactly the type of human being he despises. Roger does not fail to notice that Paule acts unusually tender toward Simon. That night, Roger takes her to bed.

Simon continues his pursuit of Paule: he invites her to lunch in the Bois de Boulogne, helps her forget about the encroaching melancholia of fall with a perfect mimicry of his mother's mannerisms, allows her to bask in his admiration and the temptation of a sexual encounter, makes a few awkward passes, and escorts her to a concert of lush Brahms music. He also chips away at her mantle of invulnerability, accusing her of having neglected the duty to be happy and condemning her to a life of solitude. He believes he has the right to speak his mind: he loves her. He *needs* her.

Meanwhile, Roger, indefatigable philanderer, embarks on a new adventure with a cunningly sexy starlet, Maisy—for him "a dirty little incommunicative object" (*AVB*, 83). Maisy does not compare, he thinks, to his "strong, intelligent and very female" Paule, whose love is "indestructible" (*AVB*, 85). Nevertheless, he spends Saturday and Sunday with the "object." A slip of the tongue alerts Paule that he did not work all through the weekend, as he had told her he would.

Roger's growing infatuation with Maisy and Simon's inspired love and patience combine to encourage Paule to put into action a painful separation from her official lover. She calls Simon back to her from his working sojourn in the provinces and, after making him miserable by a continuous emotional vacillation, chooses him over Roger. At least, she admits to herself, Simon will bring her all of himself. She tells Roger, only a phantom in her life these days, that she cannot see him any more. While several occasions had begun to signal to Roger the shakiness of his hold on Paule—the latest a dinner party in which Simon's eyes were fixed on her "like a searchlight regularly scanning her face" (*AVB*, 111)—he is still nonplussed by her decision.

The older woman–younger man idyll turns sour from almost the moment Paule and Simon consummate their desire. Having moved his clothing and himself into Paule's, Simon stops going to work, begins drinking heavily, and spends his days in bed wrapped in her discarded dresses. Now it is *he* who waits for Paule to come home. He is miserable because she does not love him. But he is also devoted to reinstilling youth and hope in her, permitting her to escape from time. However, even his unabashed admiration and his playing at being a real man cannot prevent her from overhearing and being hurt by the snide remarks of fellow diners who exclaim over the difference in their ages.

Paule is soon appalled by what she considers to be the abnormality of her situation. For her, the normal, even if unhappy and incomplete, is Roger. He is "her destiny, her master" (*AVB*, 170). Roger, too, has begun to realize that his only sense of home is with Paule. Temporary ports such as Maisy cannot provide him with the continuous sustenance he needs. He no longer likes what he sees when he looks in the mirror. He wants to be cherished again.

Inevitably, Simon, Paule, and Roger run into each other. When Paule's and Roger's eyes meet across the dance floor, they know where they belong. Paule says good-bye to Simon, who runs out of her life into the springtime. She knows that she is "saved and lost" (*AVB*, 186) even before she receives the phone call from Roger who excuses himself from their dinner plans that evening. Something has come up.

Choosing a Prison. *Aimez-vous Brahms . . .* can be read as a novel about the ravages of low self-esteem or as a study in masochism. It can also be understood as a fairly lucid portrait of what aging means for women in the contemporary Western world. As such, the novel is the story of woman's limits. And here it is crucial to understand "woman" as defined in a sexist society, that is, by her looks and by her relationship to a man.

The question addressed to the protagonist Paule and implied in the title, *Aimez-vous Brahms . . .* , translates as "Can you still love?" Or, rather, "Are you still open to romance and to life?" "Is the passion of Brahms's music a possibility in your existence?" The unfolding of the story provides a negative answer. Paule tries. She attempts to defeat time, to love as one loves before having lived nearly forty years of romantic disappointments. However, at the end of the novel she thinks of herself as old if not even older than the aging beauty she saw in her mirror at the beginning. What she has shed in the course of her adventure is not a worn-out Paule but, rather, the last vestiges of her young self. It behooves us first to ask why and then to examine how Sagan's triangular configuration subtly proposes a version of Paule's dilemma that the protagonist is incapable of interpreting but which should not escape the reader.

When, as a girl, Paule left her husband and stepped into a career, she made what she considers to be the only important decision of her life. She thought by not being tied to a man she did not love, she could be "happy" (*AVB*, 174). The energy expended in making that key decision seems, however, to have left her a prey to other men's desires. Happiness does not come from working. Her career as an interior decorator gives her no particular definition. Selecting fabrics and choosing furniture for customers *does* create a focus. Nevertheless, the job does not compensate for Roger's lack of commitment: "She could only pay attention to samples of material and to a man who was never there. She was losing herself, losing her own trace, she would never find it again" (*AVB,* 70). Paule exists because she exists with Roger. With his absence from her, time has no meaning. She feels empty of herself. She does not truly live.

Roger, on the other hand, extends himself through Paule. A whole being without a woman, with one Roger simply aggrandizes himself. He can therefore treat Maisy like an object and Paule like a possession. He, unlike Paule, never waits in an empty bed. Every bed he lies in attests to his competence as a lover. And his job connects him to a world of economic power struggles that he relishes as much as he enjoys his amorous combats. Although he returns to Paule because he believes he needs her feminine touch to stabilize him, she is not integral to his being. She represents for him a kind of maternal rock, present but not conscious.

Paule's leaving him only teaches Roger that "you have to watch out with women" (*AVB,* 185). He understands that he had gone too far and been imprudent. But Roger never considers that Paule has the right to behave as she does, that her needs are as important as his, that he operates within a privileged sphere of freedom to which she has no access. He even has the gall to forgive *her* for her "dalliance" with Simon. When he says to her, "Paule, I have so much confidence in you. So very much" (*AVB,* 87), he means, "I know you will do what I want you to do, just as I will do what I want to do."

Paule knows this too. She is far from naive about Roger or about his blindness toward her. On several occasions she sees right through his masculine presuppositions, although she almost never challenges him about them. She understands, for example, that his gesture of tearing her away from the Van den Besh party is that of "a cautious owner" (*AVB,* 113). She pardons him, however, or, rather she accepts the rapport, in part because of her tenderness toward this man who always sleeps with his hand on his heart—as if to protect himself from getting involved with anyone.

Mostly she pardons him because she does not know how else to react. Their relationship makes sense to her. It fits in with the codes of male and female behavior that she has internalized: "When Roger took her, he was her master, she was his property, he was only slightly older than she, everything conformed to certain moral or aesthetic rules" (*AVB*, 170). Paule thus appears predestined to fail in her attempt to live apart from Roger. Because Roger is the normal, the pain he causes her is more precious than the moments of happiness she shares with Simon. Indeed, Paule adopts with Simon the same patterns that she follows with Roger. However, the roles are reversed. Paule, for example, only begins to give in to Simon when his own moral fatigue reminds her of how defeated Roger makes her feel. Now it is Simon who is the "dear victim" (*AVB*, 172).

Sagan presents a Simon who is as obsessed with loving Paule as Paule has been with Roger. In fact, this Simon, far from being Roger's rival, should really be considered Paule's double. The doubling technique is apparent from the moment Paule first sees him in the mirror of the Van den Besh apartment where she had begun to examine herself. From that time Simon is constantly, if only figuratively, with her, invading her empty bed in the lovesick letters he sends and she reads in the early hours of the morning.

A reflection of Paule, Simon thinks, plots, and worries and is so paralyzed by this intellectual torment than he almost never acts. He is feminized by his fragile appearance and by his beauty, which turns him into an object for other people's rapt adoration. He, like Paule, learns to wait, huddled, significantly, in her clothes. He allows himself to become her possession. And Paule is Sagan's only female character who "possesses" a man (*AVB*, 154). Simon is as "completely desperate" (*AVB*, 152) in his surrender to Paule as she has been and will be in her submission to Roger.

Nevertheless, while Paule ultimately sees Simon's abjection as pitiable, she never permits herself to see his plight as a mirror image of her own. Instead, she chooses to see Simon as her "youth" (*AVB*, 184) or as an adolescent boarding-school chum (*AVB*, 173) and babies that part of herself. She thus misreads a paradigm that might have permitted her to draw another conclusion about her relationship to Roger as well as to Simon. Although she gives up Simon because the positions in the master-slave game they play feel wrong to her, she never questions the game itself.

Imprisoned by preconceptions, including masochism as the woman's lot and beauty as her only arm, Paule cannot age gracefully with or without a young man at her side. She accepts the inability of real men to understand women. She concurs with society when it brands her as foolish for taking pleasure in a man fourteen years her junior. Just as Simon does not revolt from a self-characterization as a "little bird with a graceless cry" (*AVB, 93*), Paule acquiesces to her martrydom on the altar of Roger's freedom.

The Confines of Irresponsibility. A quick wind invades Lucile Saint-Leger's bedroom, waking her up to the promise of the pleasures of living and beckoning her to come out and play in the company of the spring breeze. With not much of a thought for Charles Blassens-Lignières, her protector, a distinguished middle-aged businessman twenty years her senior who is sleeping fitfully in the next room, Lucile jumps into her new sports car and speeds out of Paris. Lucile lives in the present. The reserved and lucid Charles loves her for that, and for the recklessness she has brought to the two years of their life to-gether—a recklessness that also makes him fear losing her.

That evening the May–December couple dine at ruling hostess Claire Santré's, where several ill winds are blowing. Most are directed toward Antoine, the up-and-coming young editor who dares daydream in the midst of such glittering company. Charles envies him. Diane Mirbec, the wealthy socialite who considers Antoine her companion, is angered by his inattentiveness. Johnny, Claire Santré's obliging escort, sadly remembers loving a man as beautiful as the very blonde Antoine.

In the midst of this potential tumult and the exchange of delicious gossip, Antoine and Lucile isolate themselves, resembling two thirty-year-old children by their fit of uncontrollable laughter. Piqued, Diane leaves with Charles, committing a grave error of judgment. Like eager sharks, the other guests begin to feed off Diane's discomfiture. Antoine and Lucile end up spending the night talking and meandering across the bridges over the Seine. If startlingly attracted to one another, they part as easily as they had come together.

Claire's coterie meets again for an evening of theater and a late dinner at a restaurant in the Bois de Boulogne. Charles sees the longing in Lucile's eyes and suggests she drive Antoine to the restaurant in her convertible. He feigns preference for the comfort of Diane's Rolls Royce. Antoine and Lucile find themselves kissing breathlessly, desperately, in the forest on the way to dinner. They now realize they have no choice but to see each other again.

Lucile and Antoine rendezvous in the latter's cramped apartment where they make love all afternoon. When they meet later at another cocktail party, their magnetic attraction for one another almost proves embarrassing. Johnny does what he can to shield their illicit passion from Diane's observation, but he cannot spare Charles, who suffers in silence.

Lucile's immense need of Antoine's body begins to change her rapport with the world, with time, and even with her own nonchalance. Both lovers only live when they lose themselves in the intensity of an afternoon's passion. Both are astonished by the depth of their love. Lucile, after skating on the surface of life for so long, discovers that Antoine can wound her, almost destroy her, by simply arriving late at one of their assignations. Her need to be with him becomes so crushing that her once-cherished solitude now appears ludicrous.

Charles, always dignified if tortured by Lucile's physical defection, continues to count on the security he offers as a means of holding onto her. He reckons correctly that Antoine, uncompromising and possessive, will force Lucile to choose between them. After another tasteful soirée, this time at Diane's, during which the odors of spring wafting in from the balcony almost carry Lucile away, Antoine takes a first step by crassly accusing Diane of not really responding to him as a person. In his blind passion for Lucile, he does not care if he acts like a boor with his ever-gracious official mistress.

He does care, however, that Lucile refuses to take his ultimatum seriously. After a night of violent lovemaking and Antoine's recognition that his heart is sounding *la chamade,* he demands that Lucile concede defeat to him as well. But Lucile does not understand why she has to want what Antoine wants. In fact, she really *is* fond of Charles, who never asks anything of her.

Charles sends Lucile to the Riviera to try and forget Antoine, who, furious at her inability to make up her mind, has broken off the affair. While Lucile lies on the beach, ashamed of her own unhappiness, Antoine wanders about Paris, lost. A chance encounter with Johnny alerts him to what he should have known: Lucile is pining away for him. He rushes to her and they bow to the evidence of their unstoppable love. Charles, however, will be there if Lucile needs him.

Vacationing as though from reality, Antoine and Lucile spend a glorious summer in their private dreamworld, pricking their passionate unity by occasional splinters of doubt. Fall arrives and with it Antoine's realization that Lucile's ability to be happy by doing nothing for hours on end is quite monstrous. He directs her out of the apartment (in the rain and on the bus) to movies in crowded *cinémathèques.* He even gets her a job on a magazine, which she quits without telling him, cashing in her pearls for the freedom of constructing an elaborate fiction about how she spends her days doing research.

When Antoine discovers the fabrication, he is forced to admit that something is irretrievably broken between them. Lucile has already understood this and therefore decided that she cannot keep the child she is carrying. Furthermore, neither their couple, predicated on liberty, nor the child she is herself, would tolerate a baby. But Lucile cannot face the medical butcher whom Antoine has been able to procure. Only Charles has the necessary connections and money to assure her a safe abortion in Switzerland.

Thus, after her unsuccessful and silly attempt at work, the trauma of refusing the new life within her, and the realization that Charles, alone, is capable of providing those moments of ethereal beauty—music, crystal, taste, and charm—that cushion her from the onslaught of time, Lucile leaves Antoine. She senses that she is "saved and lost at the same time" (*C,* 226).

Several years later, Lucile, married to Charles, and Antoine, a prosperous editor, meet again at Claire Santré's. The dinner conversation turns to the connotation of the expression "la chamade." Neither Lucile nor Antoine gives any indication that the term once conferred meaning upon their entire universe.

Choosing Another Prison. The heroine of *Aimez-vous Brahms . . .* elects normalcy as her fate, but Lucile in *La Chamade* claims freedom. While Paule gives herself over to the female role, Lucile rejects almost everything recognized as womanly: nurturance, motherhood, companionship, caretaking, guaranteeing hearth and home, and so on. Nevertheless, in both cases, through their choices, however opposite they appear, the heroines also define their limits. Each recognizes at the end of the novel that she is not just saved but also, and more pointedly, lost. In Lucile's case, she, like the wind that has accompanied her from the beginning and throughout the development of the novel, simply stops gusting. Rather, she settles into the comforting blue-hued, blue-blooded cocoon that Charles Blassens-Lignière has kept waiting and warm. Her freedom, then, deserves close examination, for her cult of noncommitment reads more accurately like an invitation to place on her a set of disguised psychological shackles.

Charming and disinterested, basically content, orphaned as are so many of Sagan's principal characters, without work or goals, Lucile spends little time thinking about herself. Sagan tends to show her in action, that is, receiving the world, living for the moment. Charles worships her because of this ingenuousness, because she falls asleep at his side like a child who has just run out of steam, because, he thinks, she is really a "rough draft" (*C*, 103) of a human being. He knows that she, unlike himself, can savor the word "balcony" and enter into the realm of romance it implies. In Charles's eyes, Lucile overwhelms life instead of being crushed by it. And, as he caresses her black curls "that will never belong to me" (*C*, 64), he admits that he cannot truly own her. Lucile is free.

Antoine, as well as the narrator and Lucile herself, remark on her similarity to an animal who enjoys holing up in its lair (*C*, 198, 215), uncannily in tune with the elements. This subdued bestiality eventually awes and frightens Antoine: "When he saw her again, looked at that face so intact, carefree, distracted, he felt that it wasn't really a matter of shameful weakness but, rather, of profound strength, hidden and animallike, which turned her away from life in its most natural sense" (*C*, 229). Lucile, then, is not just free but also unnatural—at least for Antoine who has no difficulty defining "natural" as the contrary of a person without tags or responsibilities.

For both Charles and Antoine, Lucile is doubly distanced. Not merely the "other" to them as men, she also counters the dominant image of "woman." Lucile's nebulousness to herself, as well as to them, allows the men in her life to see her as they will: a free spirit for Charles, a monster to Antoine. Of the many ways in which they image her, the standard attributes of personhood: desires, emotional contours or direction, remain flagrantly absent.

This alternative woman opens herself entirely to only one situation—pleasure. Creature of sensation, engaged in nothing else, Lucile must respond to pleasure when it calls her. Embodied by another human being, especially the equally (if momentarily) hedonistic Antoine, pleasure dresses itself with the ineluctability of destiny. Lucile has no structures to resist its beckoning. She gives herself over totally. Together, therefore, Lucile and Antoine fuse into one: "They knew nothing of each other, but their bodies recognized one another with such fervor, such devotion, such a sentiment of the absolute, that their memory became entangled in the present, and they sought desperately but in vain to remember something precise about each other after having parted. The only living instant of their lives [was] the moment they came back together again" (*C*, 90–91). Everything—technology, time, nature—receives meaning through their passion. Returning to Paris in their sleeping-car compartment, the violence of the moving train echoes, doubles, and enmeshes itself in their crazed embrace: "It seemed to them that its speed was increasing twofold in their pleasure, that the train was going insane, and that they themselves were the ones emitting hellish moans into the sleeping countryside" (*C,* 170). Passion annuls any ability they have to analyze, scrutinize, or assess themselves or each other.

In Sagan's universe, however, as reality creeps in in the form of work and financial needs, this pleasurable intensity collapses. It cannot endure specifically for Antoine, the man who, unlike Lucile, has ambitions and projects, or, in other words, a future. And as he thinks about the future, *his* future, he tries to fit the formless Lucile within it. His superficiality, which Sagan had shown earlier in his callous and uncomprehending treatment of Diane Mirbec and in his inability to recognize Lucile's rights, reasserts itself. Like Roger in *Aimez-vous Brahms . . .* Antoine never even attempts to imagine what might be going on inside his mistress's head. Seeing her as a mute monstrosity permits him to dismiss the perplexities she represents.

Charles, on the other hand, understands too well what Lucile needs to preserve the illusion of a neverending present. Mozart and money in unbroken rhythm soothe away the poundings of *la chamade*. Giving and forgiving, this marvelous father figure never descends to the vile tactics of ordinary human beings. But then he does not have to, as his wealth and power protect him from all forms of dirt. In the image of Diane's Rolls Royce (*C,* 62), harboring the two of them and overpowering with its aura the sports car holding Lucile and Antoine, Sagan warns the reader early on about who will win this love battle and why. Charles can afford to wait for Lucile. He, a vigorous businessman, does not need her to exist but merely to broaden himself. Thanks to Lucile, he has already been able to stretch his imagination, projecting her among the seraphim.

While the material abundance, the devotion, and the idolatry Charles offers might suggest a reading of this novel as an ideal woman's fantasy, it is clear that Lucile must give up passion, the ultimate pleasure, in order to indulge all the others Charles holds out to her. The timeless state that luxury affords and that allows her to feel free is, in fact, a subtle form of slavery, as is her acceptance of Charles's notions about her. Charles may choose to believe he can never own Lucile, but her situation at the end of the novel indicates otherwise. By becoming Mme Blassens-Lignière, she merely continues to cultivate self-definition through him. Lucile surely does not belong to herself. At the novel's close, her carefreeness has lost its vital edge. It is with anguish that she admits to herself that there is no role for her in the comedy of life: "She wasn't a courtesan, nor an intellectual, nor the mother of a family, she was nothing" (*C, 242*).

Like Paule in *Aimez-vous Brahms . . .*, Lucile also acquiesces to an emotional stalemate. She too gives up the liberating potential of the unknown and forbidden for the security of the known and conventional. And like Paule's choice, Lucile's, in the context of the novel, is understandable. Given her only alternatives: nasty social climbing or striving to be the ideal helpmate, Lucile's oddly principled parasitism seems almost tolerable.

Aimez-vous Brahms . . . and *La Chamade* can both be qualified as learning-adventure stories whose lessons, nonetheless, cancel out the possibility of further emboldened undertakings. In the end, their heroines, like Dorothy in *The Wizard of Oz,* discover that "there's no place like home." However, whereas Dorothy's adventures allow her to put to rest the demons of the real world through exposing them in dream, Paule's and Lucile's escape into fantasy only shows them the penitentiary confines of their chosen reality. Paule gives up freedom for what she, through society, considers to be normal for an aging woman. Lucile clings to a phoney freedom in her attempt to run away forever from womanhood as she and society understand it. Sagan gives neither character enough energy to seek anything different than the prison she already knows or to imagine a "woman" other than one imposed by a patriarchal mentality.

The Dead-End Triangle:
Un peu de soleil dans l'eau froide

Un peu de soleil dans l'eau froide departs in two important ways from *Aimez-vous Brahms . . .* and *La Chamade* and, in fact, from Sagan's corpus in general. The first is by a juxtapositioning technique in which the author contrasts Parisian scenes with provincial, dithyrambic ones. Through this opposition Paris appears more clearly than usual in Sagan's novels a "whore" and direct rival to the Limousine character Nathalie. By this device Sagan also draws more attention to the novel of manners component, capturing both a bourgeois Limoges and a nouveau riche Paris. In her portrayal of provincial domesticity, she composes one of her rare but very appealing slapstick portraits—that of

Florent, the gauche and gesticulating brother-in-law of Gilles, the protagonist.[9]

The second departure from the Saganian romance corpus occurs in the introduction of the character Nathalie Sylvener. Even though Nathalie qualifies as a love addict, she has a greater profundity and intelligence than any of Sagan's likewise afflicted heroines, or heroes for that matter. In her remarkable culture and poise, Nathalie resembles Anne of *Bonjour Tristesse*. A true intellectual, Nathalie loves to discuss literature and the arts. She sets uncompromising standards for herself. And, as a lifelong Limousine, she has escaped, it would appear, the vanity and flightiness of her Parisian counterparts.

In other respects, *Un peu de soleil dans l'eau froide* offers more consistent examples or original variations of techniques used in all of Sagan's novels. She multiplies, for instance, the *coup de théâtre* effect. This involves positioning the narrator's summary statement, itself only obliquely related to what precedes it, in such a way as to hit the reader with an emotional bang. For example, the observation, "As for Nathalie Sylvener, she loved him as soon as she saw him" (*PS*, 68), follows on the heels of a lengthy description of Gilles's pathetic state at the end of the first dinner party he is forced to attend in Limoges. Nothing specific has prepared us for this romantic thunder bolt.

Sagan also increases the narrator's distance from the protagonists. While the main character (here Gilles) is indeed the center of consciousness, as in her earlier third-person novels—that it, what is seen in the novel is mainly filtered through his eyes—Gilles's point of view does not continuously merge with the narrator's. The narrator's comments about him grow increasingly hostile and sarcastic. From a sympathetic victim of a Sartrean-style existential crisis at the beginning of the novel, Gilles evolves into an egotistical bludgeoner. The effect is to encourage the reader to identify with the enigmatic Nathalie, even though we rarely glimpse what is happening in her mind.

Finally, as noted in the introduction to this chapter, the triangular configuration in *Un peu de soleil dans l'eau froide* includes an inhuman player—death. Nathalie's growing attraction to it, with Gilles as means, figures a triangle that can serve as a warning about woman's place in the contemporary world.

Escape from Loving. Thirty-five-year-old Gilles Lantier wakes up to wonder what is wrong with himself. He seems to be losing control of his life: he can neither take interest in his live-in companion Eloïse or in his rather enviable newspaper career. Attempting to confide in his friend Jean hardly helps. Jean maintains that the boyish, carefree Gilles is simply suffering from too many parties. And both his doctor and his ex-mistress Gilda suggest that he has but two choices: wait out the depression or kill himself. Half the population of Paris has the same problem. That evening Gilles falls apart: he beats up a boorish colleague; he bursts into tears.

He thus travels down to Limoges to the home of his sister Odile to try to recover his emotional equilibrium. Odile mothers him, while her giddy husband Florent plies him with bubbly port-wine cocktails. Yet all this, and even the beauty of an early provincial summer, cannot shake him out of his lethargy or assuage his panic. He feels like a "deer hunted by a pack of dogs" (PS, 63). Odile and Florent nearly have to drag him to dinner at the sky-blue salon of family friends. There, he meets the red-maned, intriguing, and genteel Nathalie Sylvener. Nathalie falls immediately in love with him.

Unmindful of her reputation as first lady of Limoges, Nathalie fetches Gilles the next day and cures his depression and his impotency with her goodness and candor. She claims to possess the moral absolutism of the heroines of Russian literature. If at first skeptical, Gilles soon comes to see that this willful woman is indeed remarkable—a living goddess. His jealousy of the man whom he takes to be Nathalie's lover and who turns out to be her brother alerts him to his growing passion. When he hesitates to leave Limoges after receiving a call from Jean insisting that he return to Paris to accept an even better position at the paper, Gilles knows he is hooked.

Although he does journey to Paris, Gilles cannot keep his mind off Nathalie. She, in images of prairies, waving grass, sunshine, and the poplar trees of Limoges, is all he can see. He cannot keep on living with Eloïse and tells her so. Then, he hurries back to Limoges, after apologizing confusedly to Garnier, the homosexual colleague whose place he has technically usurped in the newspaper's hierarchy. Garnier takes the blame upon himself: he has lost his promotion by proclaiming the right to love whom he chooses.

Reunited with Nathalie, Gilles is aware of fearing her integrity and her capacity to judge him almost as much as adoring her ability to give herself completely to him. As for Nathalie, she knows that Gilles adjusts his principles without difficulty, but she also knows that she cannot live without him. He is her fate: "I've led a very protected, very soft, and very boring life, she said calmly. I think that something like you was bound to happen to me" (PS, 142–43). Their rapturous afternoons of lovemaking in Gilles's attic bedroom somewhat allay his anxiety. After she leaves him, he lies folded into an old sweater, remembering her smell and her warmth. At last Nathalie's brother confronts Gilles with the necessity of taking action so as not to compromise Nathalie any longer. Gilles proposes she leave her husband and her life in Limoges and join him in Paris.

When Nathalie arrives at Gilles's two-room flat, however, her perfume "smells wrong" (*PS,* 170). It is, he thinks, a summer smell. And Nathalie does not fit in at the Club with his wise-cracking and high octane friends. Only the sad-sack intellectual among them attracts her. Nathalie prefers good books, evenings at the theater, and stimulating discussions to the night life Gilles has always known. She even suggests to Gilles that his bosom buddy Jean acts more like a bad angel than a friend, and, worse, she corrects his blowhard publisher, attacking his vanity when he incorrectly attributes a quote to Stendhal.

Although Gilles assures himself that he is still dominant in their lovemaking, he finds it necessary to act irresponsible and uncaring at the Club in order to assert his independence. Absorbed in his own games, he does not even notice that Nathalie has unwittingly captured the attentions of one of the richest fashion photographers in Paris. All while grudgingly admiring her in silence, Gilles can only complain aloud about her tastes, including her growing friendship with the idealistic Garnier.

Gilles understands neither the kind of love she and her brother share nor the part he is supposed to play when she is called back to Limoges because her dearest aunt has died. He hates the feeling of being the leashed male unleashed. And so he makes her suffer again for his own frustration, as he did once earlier, by breaking trust and spending the night away from home.

When Nathalie returns from Limoges, her spirits seem broken. Overhearing Gilles describe to Jean how she has begun to smother him, Nathalie emerges from the bedroom and calmly leaves the apartment "to run some errands" (*PS,* 244). While she is killing herself with tranquilizers in a seedy hotel, Gilles races from apartment to train station to apartment, hoping to find her. He is desperate and frightened, but time has run out.

Death, the Only Gentle Man. *Un peu de soleil dans l'eau froide* is the most bitter of Sagan's romances. The "sunlight in cold water" of the title, rather optimistic in its original version—Eluard's verse evokes a sensation of life—becomes irredeemably pessimistic in Sagan's hands. [10] Not the pain of lost love but the horror of lost life infuses the novel's "sunlight." The victim, Nathalie Sylvener, is in nearly every respect the strongest and most uncorrupted character of Sagan's repertory. Gilles calls her a repository of "peace and love" (*PS*, 137). We might ask, then, why must Nathalie die and what does Sagan tell us by her death?

Un peu de soleil dans l'eau froide can be read as the pathology of love addiction, from its incubation stage to a worst-case manifestation. Ironically, it is Gilles who wants to kill himself at the beginning of the novel. Nathalie seems to have caught the suicidal drive from him. But, in fact, he has contaminated her in another way, serving only as a catalyst for her own fatal illness. His mediocrity and unworthiness gradually engulf her. She may recognize his weakness and his bad faith, yet she has wed herself to him, and thus to what he represents: "You make believe you detest the fundamental stupidity of this century, its lies and its violence. But you live in it like a fish in water. You swim comfortably only in its midst, against the current, of course, but so very cleverly. You turn off the T.V. and the radio, that's true, but you *enjoy* turning them off. The gesture sets you apart" (*PS*, 228). Having given up all other possible definitions of herself, Nathalie loses her sense of integrity when she begins to lose respect for Gilles.

In the early stages of their affair, Nathalie admits that her life has been "simple and devastating" (*PS*, 149–50). Married to a local dignitary, childless, Nathalie has led an existence characterized by elegance and calm. This calm, however, disguises a paralyzing hysteria, the "desperation" that marks so many of Sagan's female characters. It is, in fact, only a slightly tamer version of the vacuousness that distinguishes Marguerite Duras's protagonists, such as Anne Desbaresdes of *Moderato Cantabile*. Duras's characters, like Sagan's Nathalie, emptied of themselves, without any acceptable identity, are ripe to jump into an all-encompassing passion. They die figuratively of love in a miasma of eroticism and self-defeat, thereby shielding themselves from the unbearable burden of having to be. Nathalie, through her attachment to Gilles, takes the figurative to its literal realization.

In Limoges she still has some control over her life. She has her "good works" and a social role to play that she can take seriously. She also has a brother nearby who loves her unconditionally. She can therefore appear to Gilles and to the rest of the community as intrepid and resourceful. She can make Gilles confront the truth about himself and laugh about it. She can even save him by her constancy and forthrightness. She gives form to a Gilles who, bereft of any morality of his own, is incapable of rebuilding his psyche by himself. Nevertheless, Nathalie cannot tell him what she wants and needs. She does not know how to demand. Her brother must interpret in her stead.

Once in Paris, without the social and fraternal props that have held her upright, the fragility of Nathalie's mental structure becomes obvious. Her values do her no good in a world in which values are meaningless. Gilles's milieu operates out of a circumscribed brinksmanship that encourages the triumph of mediocrity. No wonder Nathalie takes as her only men friends those people considered "losers" by Gilles's crowd. She gravitates naturally to a gay man and an alcoholic loyal to their passions at whatever cost to personal ambition.

While Gilles recognizes the shallowness of his chosen sphere and even attempts to appreciate the spirit of self-scrutiny Nathalie brings to it, he cannot change. He permits his friend Jean, operating as an "angel of death," to release that part of himself that rejects any responsibility for Nathalie's happiness. His masculinity reasserts itself in his flirtations at the Club, his drunken spree with the boys, and his cavalier attitude toward Nathalie's concern over his whereabouts. The only way he manages to withstand the pressure of her disapproval as long as he does is by reassuring himself that Nathalie remains subordinate in their lovemaking: "In an hour or two, she would be his, submissive as she would never be in any other circumstance, and that suited him amply enough" (*PS,* 187–88). Nevertheless, after a while even this sexual domination proves insufficient.

Like the male partners in *Aimez-vous Brahms . . .* and *La Chamade,* Gilles cannot understand his lover. In fact, he refuses to understand her. He lives in a mental space of such extreme egocentrism that her pain at leaving her husband and her suffering at the loss of her aunt are impenetrable to him. He can only see Nathalie in relation to himself: his full-bodied Earth Mother in Limoges, his winsome curiosity in Paris. Like Simon of *Aimez-vous Brahms . . .,* he needs Nathalie and that seems justification enough for their being together. Also like Simon, Gilles fears his woman. He, too, "shivers" because he cannot annex her, because she remains opaque to him, because, he judges obtusely, she is "perfect" (*PS,* 240).

As true of Simon too, this vulnerability renders Gilles more sympathetic to the reader than many of Sagan's male characters. Especially in Limoges, lolling for hours in bed, content to wrap himself up in Nathalie's smells, Gilles appeals by his sensitivity—a sensitivity tra-

ditionally depicted as "feminine." Back in Paris, however, all femininity vanishes. Gilles has no time to dwell on Nathalie and no desire
even to try and figure out his own motivations. His self-analyses are
constantly foiled by a power of rationalization greater than that of any
other of Sagan's characters. The narrator does not hesitate to point this
out. For example, feeling sorry for himself when confronted by the
loving and joyous reunion of Nathalie and her brother, Gilles hypocritically muses: "Solitude certainly did have its charm from time to
time. When push came to shove, he'd always been a solitary sort, a
good old solitary wolf, and [the narrator comments] it was in purring
a bit over that self-image that he fell asleep, with all the lights on"
(*PS*, 213).

Even if sickened by his prolonged adolescence, Gilles gratefully returns to it under the influence of the French capital. Moreover, he
orchestrates situations in which Nathalie is forced to scold him. She,
true to script, plays his game right up to the end, providing an excuse
for him to reject any collusion in her death by leaving a note which
declares: "It's not your fault, my darling" (*PS*, 248). Thus Nathalie,
like Paule in *Aimez-vous Brahms . . .* , if wise to whom her man is and
even to his ignorance concerning her hurt, still gives in to the desire—
suicidal in Nathalie's case—to stay with what she has, to seek no other.

Sagan shows us that Nathalie, in making the momentous effort of
leaving her husband and a conventionally defined life, has not much
energy left to keep on fighting. She also shows us that Nathalie's
switching from provincial wife to Parisian mistress, rather than a regeneration, really only refashions and deepens the same dead-end existence. No man—neither her staid and dependable husband nor her
playboy lover—can keep Nathalie alive. A man, however, is all she
knows to look for, or, rather, the only destiny Sagan allows her to
choose. Summertime in Limoges merely provides an evanescent refuge
from the reality of her crushing solitude. Death is the one "gentleman"
who will put an end to her emptiness. Nathalie runs to death's embrace
for her final and least compromising affair.

The Parthenogenetic Triangle: *Le Lit défait*

Le Lit défait is unique among Sagan's works in that it is the literary
capstone of three previous novels, beginning with *Dans un mois, dans
un an* (1957), and proceeding to *Les Merveilleux nuages* (1961) and the
first-person romance *Un profil perdu* (1978). All four novels deal with

the same characters in differing combinations. Not really fragments of a human comedy or historical saga, the post-1957 novels instead attempt to give clearer shape to the mass of givens in the first one. Only *Le Lit défait* succeeds in embodying the concern with sadomasochism— present throughout the quartet—in likable and believable characters.

Dans un mois, dans un an, with its divergent plot lines and vaguely drawn characters, introduces Josée Ash and Béatrice Valmont whose specific stories are featured respectively in *Les Merveilleux nuages* and *Un profil perdu* (Josée) and *Le Lit défait* (Béatrice). While *Les Merveilleux nuages* explores the repulsive neurotic attachment between a young Josée and her artist husband, *Un profil perdu* puts to rest Josée's story in an improbably happy fashion by marrying her off a second time to a veterinarian. This pat ending conflicts with the trajectory of the novel as a whole but does introduce a narrator whose ironic detachment (paradoxical for a first-person voice) presages that of the third-person narrator in *Le Lit défait.*

Le Lit défait takes up the Béatrice Valmont-Edouard Maligrasse-André Jolyet triangle briefly sketched in *Dans un mois, dans un an* and eliminates Jolyet as a suitor. This last novel of the series, more attuned to the social, gently puts down in tongue-in-cheek scenes an avaricious and self-involved theater and film set. Its omniscient narrator, tough on all the characters' foibles and sharing no one's point of view, also laces the narrative with succulent love maxims. Here, for example, is his comment on Edouard's naiveté: "He didn't know that what one terms 'weakness' in the beloved always elicits tenderness before revealing itself to be mortally dangerous" (*LD,* 36). Although the narrator begins *Le Lit défait* by telling Edouard's story and by keeping the reader out of Béatrice's head, in the second half of the novel Béatrice develops a startling self-consciousness. This evolution seduces the reader into understanding her position, too. Because *Le Lit défait* finally posits an enduring couple in which both man and woman achieve a viable modus vivendi through vivid use of their separate imaginations, the novel is not only unique as part of a series of novels but also exceptional among the four third-person romances basic to this study.

Loving as Acting. Béatrice Valmont and Edouard Maligrasse linger in bed after their first passionate lovemaking since their separation five years earlier. Béatrice is an actress—a superb and much touted star of the Parisian Boulevards. Edouard writes intellectual plays that have garnered the admiration of even the nonintellectual critics. Edouard can barely believe he has been readmitted to Béatrice's sensual universe. She had dismissed him before like a servant. Thus, he has returned with only one desire: to keep on serving her, a desire her voracious sexual energy allows him to fulfill until he is nearly swept away.

Reemerging into the world, the newest couple of the moment attends a flashy film gala. There they meet Tony d'Albret, Béatrice's grasping but clever agent; Kurt van Erck, Edouard's friend, an avant-garde theater director; and Nicolas Sainclaire, the parasitic but still charming actor, friend to Edouard and former lover of Béatrice. Bedecked in black sequins and plumes, Béatrice plays her evening's role of femme fatale to perfection.

Before joining his beloved torturer in Amiens where she is on tour, Edouard stops at the Jeu de Paume to slip psychologically into the blue sky of a Magritte painting. The heaven he finds there, however, contrasts sharply with Béatrice's petulant welcome. He disturbs her so much by the evident joy he takes in composing his new play that she sends him back to Paris. Edouard, however, decides that Béatrice was just trying to protect herself and rushes back to her. Meanwhile, Béatrice has had ample time to sooth her own frustrations by sleeping with her co-star. Her reunion with Edouard is therefore a happy one, taking the form of another torrid evening of love.

Edouard, back in Paris and on his way to one of Kurt's rehearsals, meditates on the importance of his new character "Frédéric" and on Frédéric's rapport with the other reality of his life, Béatrice. Kurt warns Edouard about what he deems to be Béatrice's superficiality, but Edouard only wants to follow her about town, smitten. Not without proof, Béatrice teases him later that week about his bleeding-heart liberalism, while Tony begins a transparent but successful campaign to bring Edouard into her agency's fold.

Learning that André Jolyet, the man for whom she left Edouard five years before, is dying of cancer, Béatrice determines to see him again. She is visibly upset by the news of his illness. This tender and nostalgic Béatrice frightens Edouard. He prefers to think of her as cruelly indifferent, the Béatrice, for example, who did not disguise her discomfort during his reading of a scene of his latest play.

The meeting with Jolyet turns out to affect Edouard in much the same way as Béatrice: he, too, admires the elegance and irony of the most discerning theater director in Paris. He therefore accepts gladly, as does Béatrice, an invitation to spend several days on the Riviera in Jolyet's villa. However, Edouard's enjoyment turns to stupefaction when, through Jolyet's binoculars, he sees Béatrice make love to Gino, a casual acquaintance.

Jolyet understands better than anyone why Edouard not only does not leave Béatrice after this, but also seems to relish, if unconsciously, her sexual treason. He warns the guilt-free Béatrice that she had better watch out so as not to end up performing in life Edouard's scripts. He also congratulates Edouard for his own performance. In a show of virility appreciated by Béatrice, Edouard has given Gino a bloody nose.

Kurt's latest venture proves a colossal failure and prompts both Béatrice and Edouard to recognize that, unlike Kurt, a theater artist in order to succeed has to accept compromise and even betrayal as part of his or her lot. They settle into summer and their respective projects. While Edouard writes, Béatrice learns her lines for a new film. She also replaces an ailing actress in the role that originally launched her career. On stage, confronting the only face she truly loves—the public's—she realizes she has finally begun to live again.

Edouard once more follows Béatrice and her entourage (Tony, Nicolas, and Cathy, her maid)—this time to the filming of *Besides, Perhaps,* where he acknowledges that she looks at him as though he were "a kilometric marker tumbled onto the set" (*LD,* 144). To give himself some leverage and allure, he invents, with the encouragement of Nicolas, a story about covering the filming for the American movie magazine *Show-Show.* Everyone, including Béatrice, falls for it. She also, however, falls for the phoney photographer whom Edouard has enlisted. She has indeed begun to understand that Edouard loves her precisely for this kind of indiscretion. And when she discovers his own ploy to be near her, she pronounces that his imagination, more than anything else about him, thrills her.

The film finished, Béatrice strides through the winter months, keeping the dying Jolyet company in the afternoon, refusing to pity him, discovering with him what value his pain has brought to the trivialities of life. She discovers, too, that she loves Edouard "for real" (*LD,* 205). Yet this avowal has an unsettling effect on Edouard and, thus, on Béatrice as well: "She felt her conqueror overwhelmed by his victory and she was frightened by it" (*LD,* 209).

When Edouard leaves for New York to attend the American premiere of his first play, Béatrice takes refuge in Nicolas's arms. She relearns there that the body's pleasures are something she has never denied and of which she has always felt proud. Of this and her latest adventure she tells Edouard—in a revelation which stuns him—upon his return. In the instant of speaking the words, she feels herself becoming an other, someone "uncompromising and bloodthirsty" (*LD,* 285), someone, however, without whom the stricken Edouard cannot

live. Their reconciliation is effected over a full reading of his newest
play, a work that confirms him in Béatrice's eyes as a remarkable playwright, just as she is an exceptional actress. Edouard, she knows, has
given her, along with his love, her greatest role.

Edouard Loves "Béatrice." *Le Lit défait* is a novel of extremes,
treating brutally and expressively both death and desire. It is the sex-
iest of Sagan's romances, with a racy but never objectionable lovemaking scene in almost every chapter. It is also one of her most poetically
charming. The author Sagan is more obviously present in this romance
than in any of her others. She, through the narrator, takes great delight
in playing with language, describing Jolyet, one of the most captivating secondary characters she has created, for example, as "the great
pedestrian and the great philanderer, a man infatuated with the sidewalks and the streetwalkers of his city" (*LD*, 221).

Furthermore, in *Le Lit défait* Sagan for the first time seems to divide
herself, through the narrator's loyalties, between two characters:
Edouard, the writer, and Béatrice, the actress. In fact, she once con-
fided in an interview that she felt closest to Edouard of all her creations.[11] Thus while Béatrice becomes more sympathetic to the reader
as the novel progresses, Edouard never completely loses his appeal—
not as a lover, but as a playwright plagued and thrilled by the efforts
of creation. Indeed, in this novel Sagan confers the same militaristic
images on writing as on loving: for Edouard, writing is war and words
are his "faithful allies, his troupes" (*LD*, 178). Occasional narratorial
digressions double, moreover, his concerns. These are similar to, but
much less frequent than, the remarks in *Des bleus à l'âme,* in which the
obvious authorial person, "F. S.," steps in to reflect on life and writing.

Le Lit défait may at first seem to reverse the usual pattern of a Sagan
romance, for in it the male character Edouard is the love addict, with
the female character Béatrice his torturer. For a change it appears that
the man is the victim of the love story. However, while these characterizations are initially correct, Sagan manages to work out her plot in
such a way that it becomes clear that Edouard, apparently defeated by
his love for Béatrice, actually coerces her into evolving a second self
that obeys even his most secret and humiliating desires. Thus Edouard,
the male character, does indeed control the situation. Yet the barely
disguised autobiographical component in this text, which none of her
other third-person romances possesses and which takes the form of a
dual portrait of the artist, adds another twist, giving Béatrice, as well,
a measure of control. In *Le Lit défait,* Sagan suggests that a well-

developed imaginative capacity may at least temper the male-female battle with the patina of art. Nevertheless, for the female character, the message that emerges from this solution is once again mixed.

At the beginning of the novel, the Edouard Maligrasse Sagan presents to the reader defines himself only in terms of Béatrice. He wants to suffer on the altar of love he has set up to her—his Love Goddess, his "ferocious idol" (*LD*, 25), his "sexual barbarian" (*LD*, 17). More abject than Sagan's most abject love addict, Edouard censors his conversations with Béatrice just as Paule in *Aimez-vous Brahms . . .* holds back the truth from Roger. Béatrice's bed is Edouard's reality and she is "the vampire of his life" (*LD*, 11). Shortly, however, the narrator permits us to see that Edouard's masochistic pleasure is but an Epinal projection. Edouard refuses the whole, complex Béatrice and indulges his imagination: "Without realizing it, Edouard was constructing his love like he constructed his plays" (*LD*, 42).

For Edouard, loving and writing amount to the same struggle to control the real by structuring one's own fiction. No matter what the outcome of his affair with Béatrice, no matter how much he suffers, all his love experience will feed his art—that is, as long as there is conflict. A dominated and subordinate Béatrice would destroy the imaginative constructs that fuel both his love and his writing: "[She did not realize] to what extent [Edouard] loved her when, sovereign, she summoned him to her bed at any hour and, without giving him time to undress, without touching him herself, briefly uttered the most precise commands, the most vulgar comments, and, at the end, the most satisfied insults. When she seemed to forget all about his presence, as though he were an object or a chance encounter, turning her head far away from him and into the pillow in order to stifle her cries, that's when she conformed exactly to Edouard's myth" (*LD*, 218). Every time Béatrice cheats on Edouard, every glance at another man, every sign of indifference reinforces his love for her.

The character Jolyet, a mature Saganian hedonist, considerate and wise, and a theater man himself, first sees the complex position in which her liaison with Edouard is placing Béatrice. He concludes that his own dependency on morphine, which keeps the pain of cancer out of his mind, duplicates Edouard's dependency on the myth of Béatrice. She—the Devourer, the Fascinating Wanton—protects Edouard from moving outside the realm of his imagination. And, as his imagination guarantees his profession, Edouard benefits immensely by enclosing himself within it. Béatrice, however, as Jolyet also realizes, may lose her fearlessness and her indomitable spirit through Edouard's manipulation.

"Fresh like a water color and like a challenge" (*LD*, 83), the Béatrice we see at the novel's opening, surnamed "Valmont," no doubt after Laclos's infamous seducer, is more outrageous than the most narcissistic Saganian sensualist. She exists in a constant state of desire. Like Lucile of *La Chamade,* and even more animallike than this earlier eternal adolescent, Béatrice lives only for the present. She shares the joie de vivre of Roger of *Aimez-vous Brahms . . .* and of Gilles in *Un peu de soleil dans l'eau froide.* But she is capable of much greater treachery and compassion than either of them: "as proud of her betrayals as of her altruism" (*LD*, 45). Indeed, she is the only person with enough courage and detachment to keep Jolyet company right through the moment of his self-imposed death. She never flinches or feels sorry for either of them.

By profession an actress, Béatrice constitutes the ultimate object of desire. Because a successful actress learns quickly how to please the multifaceted lover which is her public, Béatrice has acquired the knack of keeping the game of love going at her own pace. The narrator compares her offstage skills to Stendhal's La Sanseverina, who also consciously plays at life the way an actress plays on stage (*LD*, 164). Therefore, Béatrice, in the first part of the novel, rarely responds to Edouard without also seeing the scene in her mind. Her reality with her lover is one of constant stage behavior. When he threatens to suffocate her, she merely composes a camp version of herself as "female object." Or, as on the set of *Besides, Perhaps,* she reverses the rapport by surrounding herself with fetishized males, besting Edouard and most men at their own game.

Her performance mode radically changes, however, when Béatrice recognizes that she really loves Edouard. When she, too, becomes a love addict, "sucked up, dissolved, mixed within Edouard" (*LD*, 263), she nearly loses him by losing the desire to act. Nonetheless, her actress's instincts as well as her natural appetites surface again before it is too late. She understands that she must perform if she wishes to seduce her most important audience. She also realizes that the only time she does not perform is during lovemaking: "It seemed to her that that part of herself which willingly slipped into a hotel bed with [the man of the hour] was the most honest and incorruptible one" (*LD*, 174). The sleight of psychological hand she must master, then, to keep Edouard's love, involves consciously staging her "spontaneous" physical desires. In other words, she can no longer just do as she pleases, but she *must* do as she pleases in order to please Edouard. Her sexual indiscretions are as necessary to their romance as is her sexual abandonment in their lovemaking.

By Béatrice's dilemma, Sagan seems to suggest that if life can only be a role or a series of roles for women, one might as well enjoy performing them. Alone of all of Sagan's female characters in these third-person romances, Béatrice develops the particular form of self-consciousness that allows her to see herself as a character in a fiction that shapes her life. She is the only one of Sagan's third-person romance heroines who has the imagination required for play. Nevertheless, Béatrice does not conceive her own play, but rather plays out a role scripted by her lover from the only sketch of her he keeps in mind. The last glimpse Béatrice has of herself before the novel ends communicates the ambivalence of this position: "raising her eyes, she perceived her reflection in the mirror, . . . she saw [a] raven-haired woman . . . dark and . . . fatal, surrounded by . . . those early, dew-drenched, and *dead* roses . . ." (*LD,* 299; my italics). Béatrice cannot help but notice that the dewy roses, offered in a gesture of supplication by Edouard, are also dead, ripped from their soil. Encapsulated in a myth, the mirror "Béatrice," the one whom Edouard loves, is likewise truncated from herself.

Fantasy and Demystification

The Limits of Sagan's Fantasy. In a favorable if condescending critique of *Un peu de soleil dans l'eau froide,* Bernard Gros sums up Sagan's fiction as follows: "[It is] a substitute for the old-fashioned melodrama. Through it the readers fully satisfy their need to flee their own mediocrity, their emotional vacuum, the monotony of their existence. . . . [Her books] offer suffering without danger, sketch a mythological geography permitting rapid travel, and give a clear conscience without costing anything."[12] Up to a point, Gros's assessment parallels what we have seen in *Aimez-vous Brahms . . . , La Chamade, Un peu de soleil dans l'eau froide,* and *Le Lit défait.* The pleasure of fantasy and especially the imaginative freedom that fantasy makes possible are major aspects of Sagan's romances. In all four books discussed in this chapter, the reader's imagination is momentarily liberated from two of the major constraints of modern life: sexual repression and familial responsibilities. Sagan's novels neither sanctify virginity nor punish promiscuity. Characters are neither pressured to wed nor obsessed by marriage. No children, house chores, or elderly parents burden the protagonists. Especially, but not exclusively in the context of the 1950s and through the early 1970s when Sagan wrote these books, these fictional configurations were stunningly liberating.

However, not just these four but all of her romances, including the 1985 vintage, *De guerre lasse,* in which the love affair eclipses the clandestine Resistance activities as center of concern, propose a thrilling escape from the banality of the quotidian. Sagan's longtime friend and fellow novelist, Bernard Frank, stresses the allure of the escapist component of this last novel: "Her Paris under the [German] boot, her French countryside under Vichy appear as though filtered by those American films which so delighted us after the Liberation. Their falseness delivers us from evil."[13] It almost goes without saying that the filtering device in Sagan's work is always a tumultuous affair. In *De guerre lasse* the sparks fly between the Resistance fighter Anne and the happy-go-lucky industrialist Charles.

The female reader, particularly, benefits from the escape route provided in Sagan's fiction. It is the woman, after all, who is most enslaved by sexual prohibitions and housework or parental duties. Sagan's universe, devoid of both the family and the frightening bureaucracies, organizations, and political or economic minefields of the masculine arena, would seem to be designed to appeal precisely to women readers. Her novels, as Rachel Brownstein points out about literature destined for women, prepare women to live out in fiction the only adventures available to them.[14]

Yet, as we have also seen, even these fictional adventures prove disastrous for their heroines, or at best in the example of Béatrice in *Le Lit défait,* qualified. We must, then, take issue with Bernard Gros who claims that Sagan's novels offer "suffering without danger." Her romances are only harmless to the woman reader if she does not accept the fictional ending as the only attainable destiny for women and if, even while enjoying the seductive vision of erotic unicity, she permits herself to contemplate the hidden and not so hidden questions concerning woman's fate. To quote Brownstein again, these texts "are full of useful information [if women] would try to change."[15] Reading Sagan for an emotional catharsis, while certainly pleasurable, not only helps perpetuate a patriarchal status quo but also ignores crucial implications embedded in her texts.

Demystifying Women's Fate.   In the novels we have studied and in her romances in general, Sagan debunks, albeit indirectly, the possibility of resolving female destiny by choosing another so as to choose a self. Her romances reveal the fearful complexity of attempting to combine intimacy and identity. They show that burying existential being or separateness in erotic union cannot endure: perfect, immutable love is a fantasy for Sagan's characters as well as for her readers.

With this in mind, it is instructive to look more closely at the theme of solitude prevalent in all her third-person romances. In the lyrics to her love songs as well Sagan expresses the individual's desire to conquer solitude through another: "Solitude, of your promises / All that remains is smoke / . . . / I hoped one day I'd leave you / For someone whom I'd love / Someone who'd look after me."[16] In her third-person romances, all her female characters likewise desire transcendence through catapulting themselves into a love affair. They all, however, as Simone de Beauvoir might have predicted, end up alone—or worse, as in the suicide of Nathalie Sylvener. The women characters do not even have the friends and colleagues their male counterparts enjoy.

Perhaps—and taking a clue from our own reading of her earliest first-person romances—this state of aloneness should be understood more positively than the way in which the characters themselves entertain it. Sagan, indeed, through the characters' evolution and through her narrators' comments, hints at a less hesitant attitude. Paule and Lucile may be alone at the end of *Aimez-vous Brahms . . .* and *La Chamade*, but they do at least recognize their position. Contrary not just to their partners but to all the male characters, regardless of the slippage in typology between male and female, eternal adolescent and love addict, only the women characters at the end of each novel know who they are and also how they are perceived. Furthermore, they, unlike the male mythologues, do not attempt to contain their lovers in myths. Their consciousness has been painfully raised.

In a telling passage in *La Chamade*, the narrator, reflecting on Lucile's past life, even suggests that solitude might provide a true source of unadulterated elation: "Sometimes in solitude there are moments of perfect happiness, which, when recalled in times of crisis, more than any memory of another person, can save you from despair. Then you know that you really have been happy, alone, and for no reason. You know that it's possible. And happiness—which seems so tied to someone when you've been hurt by him—so irrevocably, organically dependent on him—looks to you once again like something smooth, round, intact, and forever free" (*C,* 120–21). Béatrice and Edouard in *Le Lit défait* experience this gratuitous joyfulness and their happiest moments

together in a long period of "shared solitude" (*LD*, 141). Each is completely absorbed in his or her own creative activity.

In this same novel, Jolyet's death—central to the elaboration of the
plot and the evolution of the reader's rapport with Béatrice—relativizes
the importance of erotic love and transcendence through an other. In
dying, Jolyet comprehends that the most fascinating and challenging
other is, in fact, oneself: "Sometimes I marvel—me who has been attracted to everything in life except onanism—at the possibility of putting my own hand on my own cheek and I stay amazed . . . as I have
never been by anybody else's body" (*LD*, 195). For Jolyet, the real
battle is life, not love. He fights to stay alive and his own body constitutes the only legitimate battleground. Certainly in Béatrice's doubling of herself, an operation that intrigues her almost as much as
Jolyet's continued living absorbs him, Sagan suggests the possibility
of thriving in a solitude imagined as other than a prison or an
emptiness.

While this understanding of solitude helps project her heroine's fate
in a different light, it is also illuminating to mention what options
Sagan leaves out of her third-person romances: for example, commitment to community, woman-to-woman bonding, the positive aspects
of child rearing, professionalism (other than Béatrice's acting, in certain ways the inevitable women's "profession"), or even a different conception of love, one based on equality. She intimates the latter, but
confines it to the love known only to brother and sister in *Un peu de
soleil dans l'eau froide:* "There was a kind of reciprocity between them
made up of mutual gratitude, the memory of a thousand small kind-
nesses given and received, of a thousand pleasures shared with no particular expectations" (*PS*, 212). Sagan excludes the potential for love
between a man and a woman based on partnership and presence. She
posits, instead, like the poets who provide the titles for many of her
novels, erotic desire subtended uniquely by absence. Her romantic pes-
simism, at least in these novels, seems to prevent her from envisaging
other solutions to woman's fate.

If, in her third-person romances, Sagan does not imagine any kind
of nondestructive love or any independent heroines prepared to live life
on their own, she does imagine heroines who learn from the fiction
they read. In *La Chamade,* while the men read *Le Monde* (the world),
Lucile reads Faulkner's *Wild Palms* and finds a justification for her own
radical behavior in it. Béatrice wonders aloud if she is playing *Chéri*

with Edouard (*LD,* 24). She, especially, never loses sight of the possible entanglements between life and literature.

Sagan demonstrates that she, too, has been a good reader, notably of Colette and particularly of Colette's *Chéri.*[17] She multiplies references to this novel in all of the romances discussed here, with the exception of *La Chamade.* Not only, for example, do Gilles, Simon, and Edouard, like Chéri, seek solace in sundry metaphorical wombs of maternal figures, but Gilles, again like Chéri, attempts to disappear from reality into the den of a courtesan. And while Chéri plays with Léa's pearls, Simon, the character most like him, a beautiful male object, attaches himself to Paule, the equivalent of Chéri's Léa, by a different umbilical cord—her scarves. Nevertheless, if certain of the male characters bear a disconcerting resemblance to Colette's feminized dandy, Sagan's women have, after close inspection, little in common with Léa, the "Lioness," whose bed extends her power rather than representing her vulnerability, as it does with Paule. Thus, while at the end of *Chéri* Léa achieves a victory over aging in the reaffirmation of her selfhood, Paule in *Aimez-vous Brahms . . .* only manages resignation to middle-aged incarceration, delimited by Roger's absence. As writer, Sagan has ignored or rejected Colette's vision in creating the fictional universe of her third-person romances.

No doubt Sagan's is an honest appraisal of women's limits in patriarchy, and certainly so in the postwar period in which she commenced her career, before a reinvigorated women's movement began to reexamine not only the definition of "woman" but also, for example, the contributions of writers like Colette. Colette presents unconquerable female characters who possess the intelligence and requisite sense of humor to take joy in the elusive substance of living. While this profile fits Sagan, the person, it does not characterize the heroines of her third-person romances, mired in the contradictions of patriarchy. Nevertheless, as we have noted, her characters *do* see their situation even if they cannot envisage a way out. The reader, on the other hand, is not so constrained. She—and he—taking the clue from Béatrice and the other readers in Sagan's novels, can contemplate the rapport between literature and life. The reader does not have to settle on models that define boundaries rather than possibilities.

Chapter Four

Boulevard Drama and the Pleasures of Escapism

The Sagan Romance versus the Sagan Play

The romances of Françoise Sagan confirm the way in which we tend to imagine the world—and are "popular" in that sense—but also contain subversive elements that challenge our understanding of how the world turns. While her fantasy plots often reassure, unsatisfactory or disappointing endings, a haunting melancholia, social satire, and, sometimes even an overt parody of popular genres require the reader to think about or refocus attention on how he or she fathoms "reality" and, moreover, how literature effects this process. Nevertheless, in their essential structural coherence, Sagan's romances do not suggest, as does the "new novel" of, for example, Robbe-Grillet or Claude Simon, a fragmented self or psychosocial disarray. Their central narrative concern remains, for the most part, the love story; their major preoccupation, the psychological probing of the lovers.

Satirical portraits and lyrical passages that linger over natural beauty function primarily in Sagan's novels to isolate the lovers in order to demonstrate their special sensibilities. Seductive voicing techniques, sometimes encouraging the reader to identify with the first-person narrator, sometimes aligning him or her with the superior knowledge and charming observations of a third-person commentator, establish throughout the corpus a mood or tone that brings pleasure by its sweetness and by its recognition of the bearable—if only just—weariness of human existence.

Tone also constitutes one of the more salient and endearing characteristics of Sagan's theater. Given how a theater piece generally develops, that is, by exteriorizing a conflict between two or more characters, narrators and voicing techniques usually play no role in setting the tone. (Brecht's epic theater as well as the character of the stage manager who acts as narrator in Thornton Wilder's *Our Town* are well-known exceptions.) Rather than a matter of narrative manipulation, tone in dramatic representation stems from the dialectic of the rhythm of the dialogic exchange and its semantic content. A quick repartee about the death of God, for example, creates quite a different ambience than the same-paced chitchat about what dress to wear to dinner. Stage action may, of course, also contribute to the mood.

In Françoise Sagan's case the lightness that dominates the tone of her theater is due almost exclusively to the rapidity of the characters' exchanges combined with the "social conversation" that best describes them. Her characters speak mainly to keep the contact flowing. She herself chooses to define theater in this sense: "A play is a game of ping pong."[1] And critic Jacqueline Piatier chides Sagan, in a pastiche of Verlaine, for lamenting about not writing verses. Piatier chirps, "There is nothing in [Sagan's language] that is weighty or wooden."[2] For Piatier, Sagan's delicate touch is poetic. In theatrical terms, this translates as high-style banter.

Like her romances, each of Sagan's nine plays includes a love interest, but unlike the novels none is chiefly focused on the psychology of love. This is not surprising as psychological analysis is less the province of drama than of the novel. Instead of dissecting motivations through its dialogue, theater, in fact, usually shows psychology "in action." Failing to do so, Sagan's 1979 play, *Il fait beau jour et nuit*, foundered in part because of the labored employ of psychoanalytical observations in its closing scenes.

Normally Sagan makes use of the love interest to provide a frame within which to structure her play. Her endings may conform to the comedic archetype of lovers finally getting together (or back together) and of order being restored, but the conflict is never as simple as the conventional comedy's preoccupation with overcoming an obstacle—be it family, social standing, or importunate suitor—to the union. In Sagan's dramatic conception, love turns out to be more of a means than a goal, and the restored harmony at the play's close is often a wacky one.

Again like her romances, Sagan's plays have a certain tidiness to them. Their form does not call into question the structure of reality or the ability of language to articulate it, as do, for example, the works of Ionesco and Beckett. Nonetheless, like the romances, her theater pieces, particularly the finest and most successful—over 600 first-run performances each—*Château en Suède* (Castle in Sweden, 1960) and *Le Cheval évanoui* (The stunned horse, 1966), do possess subversive components. Indeed, the inscription of a topsy-turvy world within the rigid confines of the bourgeois living rooms and parlors that comprise the spatial frame of Sagan's theatrical universe, permits both a definite dramatic tension and implies a criticism of the repression inherent in the dominant social class. In this, her theater resembles the comedies of the great masters of Boulevard drama, Feydeau and Noël Coward.

What is Boulevard Theater?

The term "Boulevard theater" dates back to the nineteenth century and conflates the type of drama with the location in which it was and frequently still is performed. About fifteen major theater houses, built on the Italianate plan (multitiered seating and a proscenium stage), such as the Porte Saint Martin and the Gymnase, sprang up or back to life on Right Bank Parisian boulevards after 1815, thereby facilitating the production of both the well-made plays of Eugène Scribe and romantic dramas. Increasingly as the century progressed, these theaters gave preference to the problem plays of Emile Augier and Alexandre Dumas, *fils*.

Although Boulevard houses, especially those on the Boulevard du Temple, known familiarly as the "Boulevard du Crime," also produced melodramas, the type of exaggerated and clear-cut conflict between good and evil that characterizes the melodramatic genre is not today considered Boulevard theater. Boulevard theater has, rather, become synonymous with a specialized dramatic structure—the superbly oiled articulation perfected by Scribe—and with a particular ideological content—one that reinforces the values and myths of the bourgeoisie, just as Dumas's plays did. Therefore "Boulevard drama" often means "bourgeois drama," both in terms of its concerns and the audience it attracts. A contemporary American equivalent would be the sentimental and deftly drawn Broadway comedies of Neil Simon whose plays preserve and cherish the ideals of "dear old Dad" (even if he is a drunkard), romantic love (even if the lovers have nothing in common but kissing and starry eyes), and marriage (even if the couple turns out to be two men—not, it goes without saying, homosexual). It is interesting to note that while several nineteenth-century Boulevard houses continue to thrive in the twentieth century,[3] those on the Boulevard du Temple, which attracted working-class audiences in droves, were torn down by Baron Haussman in his end-of-the-century renovation of Paris.

Not all Boulevard theater reassures the ruling social class and upholds the reigning morality. As noted earlier, Feydeau, for example, whose triangular or "bedroom" farces have been standard Boulevard fare since 1890, exposes the seamy underside, or "collective unconscious," of what strict middle-class social and sexual discipline has repressed. His plays offer a vision that approaches insanity. However, as Eric Bentley has shown, such stage madness might also be understood as a temporary means for the audience to break loose and enjoy what is forbidden in everyday life.[4] A Feydeau farce would, then, function as a safety valve rather than a Molotov cocktail.

In the twentieth century, theater people have argued loudly and often about the merits of various notions of theater as well as about the public to whom theater should be addressed. Avant-garde artists have scorned Boulevard theater and bourgeois drama and have helped develop small arts theaters for experimental work that challenges, among other things, the well-made play structure. Politically committed writers, actors, and directors have favored bringing theater pieces, often with a message, to a lower-middle- and working-class public in a format it can easily afford. Their efforts have been responsible for the growth of state-subsidized houses.

In the fray, Françoise Sagan has had no difficulty situating herself among the ongoing proponents of Boulevard theater, and, thus, of private houses, costly productions, and expensive tickets: "Theater is, of necessity, outmoded, and all these theories about 'the new theater' sound like hot air to me. Theater is a fundamentally bourgeois art, since a ticket costs at least twenty francs [in 1987, 120 francs—$20— for a nonsubsidized seat]. And the red, the black, the gold, the sets, the staging, everything works with the precision of marionnettes, except for *maisons de la culture* [subsidized houses] where Brecht or Pirandello is inflicted on unfortunate humans, exhausted after a day of work—which I find horrifyingly snobbish" (*R,* 97).

Sagan not only heaps ridicule on theater destined for "the people," but also gently satirizes what she sees as the excesses of the theater of noncommunication introduced in the 1960s. Here is her parody of the style:

> *She:* Where do you want to go? . . . You have no ticket, for nothing, you have no ticket for life, you don't even have one for the bus! . . .
>
> *He:* It's true, I have no ticket, I never had a ticket, I'm a man without a ticket. . . .[5]

All theatrical pretentiousness, at least what she deems pretention, provokes a scathing remark. Sagan thinks theater errs when it becomes

too "thoughtful." Several of the twentieth-century's seminal productions, contemporary with her own—Peter Brook's direction of Jean
Genet's *The Balcony* (1960), Beckett's *Happy Days* by the Company
Renaud-Barrault (1963), and the Théâtre du Soleil's *1789 ou la Révolution doit s'arrêter à la perfection du bonheur* (1789 or The Revolution
must stop at the perfection of happiness, 1971)—have had, then, no
influence on her work.

Nevertheless, it would be unfair and unintelligent to expect Sagan
to tailor her idea of theater to another author's or theater troupe's.
Furthermore, even if she does make fun of "serious" theater, Edouard
Maligrasse, the likable hero of her novel *Le Lit défait,* and most probably an alter ego, is an intellectual playwright whose plays attempt to
disturb the complacency of his public. And three of her pieces—an
adaptation of Tennessee Williams's *Sweet Bird of Youth* (1971), *Château
en Suède,* and *Un piano dans l'herbe* (A piano on the grass, 1970)—were
selected for production by the director of the Atelier, André Barsacq,
a man who has been committed since 1940 to innovative playwrights
such as Anouilh and Claudel and to plays that reject Boulevard fluff
and the bourgeois drama's tendency to muffle the female characters,
valorize only heterosexual ties, and incorporate individuals within couples as the only sign of personal success.

Sagan's Plays and Productions in the Context of the Boulevard

In the years between 1959 and 1987, Sagan wrote and had produced
on the Boulevard nine plays and one adaptation, the quite successful
and faithful version of Williams's *Sweet Bird of Youth.* With the exception of *Bonheur, impair et passe* (Win, draw, and pass, 1964) and *L'Excès
contraire* (Precipitous pleasure, 1987), all of her plays are contemporary
drawing-room comedies. *Bonheur, impair et passe* and *L'Excès contraire,*
like *Le Sang doré des Borgia* (The golden blood of the Borgias, 1978), a
cape-and-sword melodrama she wrote for television, have historical settings—turn-of-the-century czarist Russia and imperial Vienna—and
thus allow her to indulge a taste for period costumes and flamboyant
characterizations, including military officers, duelists, and unfulfilled
or insatiable great ladies.)

Sagan's career as a woman of the theater has brought upon her as
much blame as praise. She admits this merrily in the essay "Théâtre"
in her 1983 memoirs. In it, she recounts that her initial encounter

with the theater took on the emotional quality of a lark: André Barsacq, having discovered an early sketch of *Château en Suède,* convinced her to finish the play for him. She gamely took on the challenge by retreating to a ski chalet to complete the text in a few weeks. After the play's triumph in 1960, Sagan wrote *Les Violons parfois* (Sometimes violins, 1961) for the renowned tragedian Marie Bell and her theater, the Gymnase. The production failed miserably, but the experience sparked an exemplary friendship between Bell and Sagan. Only the superb performance of Danielle Darrieux as "Valentine" saved Sagan's next play, *La Robe mauve de Valentine* (Valentine's mauve dress, 1963), while the virtuosity of Daniel Ivernal as "Louis" similarly kept alive the 1970 production of *Un piano dans l'herbe.* And if *Il fait beau jour et nuit* (1978) struggled to hold the boards for the minimum union run of thirty days, Sagan barely missed total disaster by directing herself *Bonheur, impair et passe.* Several of her dearest friends—Juliette Gréco, Jean-Louis Trintignant, and Daniel Gélin—held leading roles. With Sagan at their sides, they researched Russian culture by downing shots of vodka at the bar nearest the theater. One suspects that the last minute help of director Claude Régy reestablished what coherence there was to the production.

As if to spite this mediocre record, *Château en Suède* (1960) and *Le Cheval évanoui* with the accompanying curtain raiser *L'Echarde* (The splinter, 1966) had initial runs of over two years each. They received as much acclaim from the press as from the public. After seeing *Château en Suède,* for example, *Le Monde's* Bertrand Poirot-Delpech reports sharing with filmmaker René Clair the observation that Sagan had modernized Musset.[6] Reprised in 1968, *Château en Suède* as well as the still running *Le Cheval évanoui* were two of the main hits of the Boulevard—up until the student demonstrations and political upheavals of May that forced theaters to close. It is curious and no doubt telling that Sagan's greatest successes corresponded to the period in which Brecht and Brechtianism, that is, politically concerned theater, was vying with and winning out over the "theater of the absurd" to become the most important influence on developments in French theater off the Boulevard of the 1970s.

Quite unlike experimenters of the 1970s and of the 1980s, Sagan has frequently spoken of the lack of freedom in theater. She always admits, however, to being grateful for what she believes to be its constraints: "Its tracks pilot you along by force: unity of time, unity of place, the impossibility of stopping the action under threat of boring the public, the necessity of being rapid, of rushing toward a denouement instead of languishing in sentimental daydreams, the imperious need to be nervous and convincing" (*S*, 119). This notion of how theater works and, therefore, of how it must be constructed conforms perfectly to the Boulevard model.

It is thus predictable that, generally speaking, Sagan adheres to most Boulevard conventions: a plot structure consisting of a well-articulated three-part division into exposition, development, and denouement, with the resolution following a crisis or climactic scene, and a number of surprises (or *coups de théâtre*) along the way; a relatively controllable but not too restricted cast of characters (three to four principals with as many secondary types) from a certain milieu (upper middle class, ranging from landed gentry to decadent parvenus) in certain proportions or relationships (frequently one or two servants as comic relief, always a triangular liaison underlying the drama—although not necessarily serving as crux of the conflict); a titillating situation or situations to be resolved (adultery, incest, older women with younger men), and slightly risqué characters to add piquancy (gigolos and kept women); an unchanging and enclosed spatial frame (an elegant salon, a hotel room); and a time frame that develops linearly and therefore does not stretch inordinately the boundaries of the imagination (from several weeks to a year, with leaps in time marked by blackouts between scenes or acts).

Like that of most Boulevard drama, Sagan's dramatic language is marked by fast-paced repartee and an absence of long monologues or awkward asides. Her theater practice and the conventions of Boulevard theater that inform it highlight recognizable characters and situations, emphasize materiality, and refuse overt metaphoricity or metaphysical speculation. Her plays, as is typical of Boulevard drama, start in the middle of an ongoing action, and therefore presuppose a preexistent real or an outside referent. They are not self-contained or self-reflexive entities.

Just as Sagan pays heed to a majority of Boulevard conventions in the construction of her plays, she also depends on the trappings of the typical Boulevard production to attract a sizable audience. In fact, she has never done without the number one requisite of Boulevard success: a star-studded roster of actors who subscribe to an acting style dependent on big effects, stagey manners, and loud, persuasive diction. All of Sagan's casts have included veteran Boulevard comedians and often at least one rising screen star. Philippe Noiret, for example, a French-style Walter Matthau, much-admired for his cinema work as well as his stage performances, created the role of Hugo in the original version of *Château en Suède*. A highly skilled technical actor and an expert at realizing the kind of distancing necessary to Boulevard theater in general and Sagan's plays in particular, Noiret embodied a "Hugo" who at times provoked the public to identify completely with the character. At other moments, however, Noiret, the actor, would allow the audience to see his "self," a different man from the character being played. Thus, in the fashion of superb Boulevard performances, the audience's pleasure was doubled through involvement with the actor as well as with the character.

Sagan's productions benefit not only from the charismatic talent of actors like Noiret but also from the metamorphoses effected by professional designers who turn plays produced on the Boulevard into visual extravaganzas. Each production of a Sagan play has evoked a world of wealth and glamour. Marc Bohan of Dior, for example, after already having stitched his hallmark into Valentine's mauve dress *(La Robe mauve de Valentine)*, designed the *haute-couture* wardrobes for *Le Cheval évanoui*. Celebrated hair stylist Alexandre confected coiffures for the production. And Pierre Simonini, a brilliant student of the Italian metaphysical painter DiChirico, realized a lavish set inspired by the gilded Napoleon III decor of the Rothschild family's Château de Ferrières.

Finally, Sagan's plays, like most Boulevard productions, generate and profit from the type of publicity usually reserved for high-budget films. Her opening-night galas, as well as the entire process of casting, rehearsing, and performing have been repeatedly documented. Journalist Henry Rabine, for instance, depicts appropriately through a theatrical metaphor the first-night excitement of *Le Cheval évanoui*: "Sagan sounds the three blows [which in France frequently signals the beginning of a play]. And right away the curtain goes up. On the Tout-Paris. Everybody who has a name is there. Everybody who's furious at not having one, too."[7] As if to proffer camp proof of Rabine's observation, Yves Saint-Laurent and his entourage graced the revival of *Château en Suède* by wearing the same sort of elegant eighteenth-century costumes as the characters. Myriad newspaper and magazine articles, especially in the glossy press—*Jours de France, Paris Match,* or *Elle*—show Sagan dining and cavorting with the stars of her plays. Women's magazines, in particular, ask worriedly if Marie Bell, Danielle Darrieux, Juliette Gréco, and their playwright Françoise Sagan can find happiness in their latest theatrical endeavors.[8]

All the hoopla of the Boulevard tends to subsume the play itself under a more grandiose notion of spectacle. Each of Sagan's productions, especially because of her mythic status, has attained the proportions of an "event." In this sense, alone, we can speak of Sagan as a "popular dramatist," because the entire production of a Sagan play, thanks to its material extravagance and the publicity it attracts, becomes grist for the popular imagination's mill. However, as mentioned previously, the author herself acknowledges that the average French person, though he or she can afford a Sagan novel or even a dramatic text, can ill afford an evening of Saganian theater—unless the play were to be reproduced, as three of them have been, on television.[9] A Sagan production, then, "one of those not to be imitated Parisian phenomena," to quote Elsa Triolet,[10] is an elegant gift that only the Boulevard can propose and only the upper middle class can afford to buy.

Having recognized the limited potential of Sagan's theater to attract a broad-based audience, precisely because it conforms to the mode of production of the Boulevard, we can, nevertheless, determine the ways in which her works bend and stretch Boulevard conventions. Sagan's plays depart, most importantly, from Boulevard theater's underlying premises, themes, and structural priorities. This iconoclasm confers upon her theater a specific cachet.

In the first place, her plays do not, as is typical of Boulevard drama, contain a moral directive (either expressed or implied) that reinforces the prevailing political order and moral code. As in her novels, the characters operate within the realm of amorality. Charlotte of *Les Violons parfois* signals their ethical posture: "I hate martyrs, intellectuals, gossips. I love people all curled up in their armchairs, people who know the price of caviar and don't give a damn about the price of a loaf of bread."[11] With the exception of the rather stereotypical "bad guys" in the melodramatic *Il fait beau jour et nuit*, no other characters pay for their crime, whether it be the exploitation of a rich patsy *(Les Violons parfois)*, murder *(Château en Suède)*, or repeated adulteries *(La Robe mauve de Valentine)*.

Second, although there is a semblance of order restored at the end of each play in the form of lovers or families joining together or reforming, the underlying ethos does not entail, as does most Boulevard theater, confidence in a system based on the family unit. The reestablished family at the end of *La Robe mauve de Valentine*, for example, sees Valentine returning to her husband after yet another, and clearly not the ultimate, escapade—this time with her twenty-year-old second cousin. Said young man, at last initiated to the true perils of life, attempts to find comfort with a mother who could not have cared less about witnessing her son being "used" by darling Valentine. Moreover, the mother (Valentine's first cousin) looks forward herself to an adventure with Valentine's husband. "Families" may hold the plays together by encompassing the action, but Sagan indicates that the ties that bind are very tenuous indeed.

In fact, rather than establishing a hierarchically organized or otherwise connected family, Sagan almost exclusively creates characters who resemble, even when grouped together, as critic Pierre Macabru remarks, eternal adolescents in revolt.[12] They are grown-up but still somehow pubescent, like Valentine who represents a refusal to submit to life's tedium or like Eléonore and Sébastien (*Château en Suède*), graceful parasites on aristocratic bounty.

In another variation of this most typical of Saganian theater types, an older and more resigned character, such as Henry-James (*Le Cheval évanoui*) or Louis (*Un Piano dans l'herbe*), assuages his or her former idealism with alcohol and blunt remarks. Sagan allows this variation the only meaning-laden speeches of her entire theater corpus. Louis, for example, delivers this apologia for his life: "Let me point out to you that all the shimmering and amber liquids with which I've surrounded my life were destined to protect me from you, the adults. If here I am at forty-five, broken-down, ruined, and alcoholic, it's because I've held on to my innocence right up to here, glass by glass, so I wouldn't have to listen to your schemes for money and ego gratification."[13]

The last and strangest variation of the eternal adolescent type is *le naïf*, pure in heart and simple in spirit—like Giraudoux's gardener in *Electra*—who has no ambition and makes no demands (Léopold in *Les Violons parfois*, Paul in *Il fait beau jour et nuit*, Lucien in *L'Echarde*, Frédéric in *L'Excès contraire*, or the blithely crazy Ophélie in *Château en Suède*). Like all the eternal adolescent types, *le naïf* functions in a sphere so private and narcissistic that the demands or compromises basic to a family unit only exist, if they exist at all, as a game to be played if the character feels like it.

Sagan contrasts these eternal adolescents with "the strong man" or "energetic grande dame" figure (Jean-Lou in *La Robe mauve de Valentine*, Hugo in *Château en Suède*, Charlotte in *Les Violons parfois*, Anaïs in *L'Excès contraire*, and Maud in *Un piano dans l'herbe*). However, while such a foil helps generate the conflict and creates suspense, the strong man/woman eventually ends up challenged or changed by the eternal adolescent and thankful for partaking in the state of suspension which is the adolescent's home territory. The strong man/woman, too, finally wants what the adolescent wants—freedom from any constricting familial role.

In two of Sagan's latest plays, a new "strong" type emerges, "the conniving bitch," who incarnates moral ugliness: Sylviane in *Un piano dans l'herbe* and Doris in *Il fait beau jour et nuit*. Fortunately, the stereotypical coloration of these two characters is rare in Sagan's theater. And, furthermore, the character of "the bitch" no matter how mature or controlling she appears to be, can hardly compensate for the absence of other family members. One character who comprehends the functioning of hierarchy does not a family make.

Related to the absence of the central unifying family and plethora of self-involved character types are the major themes (or motifs) that occur from play to play. This is the third domain in which there is divergence from the Boulevard model. Of key significance is the baroque-cum-modern concept of life as a series of roles and performances with, however, no corresponding obligation to perform them. Maud *(Un piano dans l'herbe)* expresses well the characters' consciousness of life as a traveling circus, and not a joyous one at that: "You can't imagine the number of cities, faces, gestures, words of love there are on this little planet. You know, I can say 'I love you' in eight languages" *(PDH,* 67). All of *L'Echarde* paints the advantages of living out a fictional role rather than coping with "reality," in whatever dull or painful form it takes. Those eternal adolescent types who are jolly, such as Eléonore and Sébastien *(Château en Suède),* as well as those who are damned, as is Henry-James *(Le Cheval évanoui),* play out their self-selected personnages. What else can they do—except conform to a role that someone else has thrust upon them? Only *le naïf* escapes role-playing. *Le naïf* seems to body forth a lost paradise, occulted by the necessities of material existence. Nostalgia for this lost Edenic haven is, then, another recurring theme throughout Sagan's theater.

Yet one path does exist to retrieve a kind of purity and wholeness—love. Love as transformative emotion is the last of Sagan's conspicuous themes. As alchemical as it is, however, love merely relocates a space of freedom from role-playing for a precious moment. Vladimir, the cad-turned-adoring lover in *Bonheur, impair et passe,* says as much to the woman with whom he has just consummated his passion: "Thanks to you, I will {at least} have been close to my own life for two hours."[14]

Not restricted to Sagan's younger characters, the "passionate illusion" often better serves the older ones. In the several instances where she pits a sensitive older generation against unimaginative or angry youth in the pursuit of love, Sagan seems, for a change, to bend to topicality. By flattering her mainly middle-aged, middle-class audience, she sides with their position in the explosive generational conflict that disrupted the late 1960s.

Despite this minor concession to a Boulevard frame of mind, Sagan does not usually pander to her audience's prejudices, nor does her theater comply with the Boulevard model in terms of the relative importance of its main components. Sagan skews the expected rapport between plot and dialogue and between dialogue and stage action. The typical well-made play privileges plot over every other element, even if this means inconsistencies in characterization and a heightened dependency on coincidence to pull everything together. Although Sagan's plays are unquestionably based on the well-made pattern, nothing much actually happens in them. Plot gives way to dialogue.

Like a good many Boulevard-type dramas, "the action" does commence in Sagan's theater when an outsider invades the family's (or ersatz family's) territory. The arrival of Frédéric in *Château en Suède,* of Léopold in *Les Violons parfois,* of Valentine in *La Robe mauve de Valentine,* for example, sets the conflict in motion. However, from that point, the pattern of ups and downs in the fortunes of the protagonists that normally governs the well-made play's development and maintains the dramatic tension and thus the public's interest is replaced by the breezy cross talk and cleverness of the dialogue. Verbal jousting and wordplay eclipse "the action," that is, the plot complications and reversals, as in the following exchange from *La Robe mauve de Valentine*:

> *Valentine:* I'm very upset.
>
> *Marie:* Don't worry; it'll blow over.
>
> *Valentine:* You're taking it well.
>
> *Marie:* I know you, you see. Me—well—life, you know, I've always clung onto it. My nature. But, you, you're a glider. Even when you were little, you had that ability. Not pretty, really, but so light. It was my dream then, to be able to glide. I only understood afterwards that for me, love, for instance, meant weighing, grabbing hold, proceeding cautiously, heavy words, business words. Oh I envied you!
>
> *Valentine:* But I've glided too much, you know; I've gone into a tail spin. [15]

Valentine's dilemma attracts the spectators' empathy not by eliciting their concern over its perilous immediacy, but by charming them through Valentine and Marie's rendition of the problem in sustained imagery of "gliding" and "lightness."

That master of doing through speaking, Sébastien, from *Château en Suède,* in explaining his attitude to Hugo, touches upon the spirit that informs Sagan's preference for witty dialogue over convoluted plot:

> Hugo: . . . What pleasure do you take in making fun of another man?
>
> Sébastien: The lowest, Hugo, therefore one of the most profound.
>
> Hugo: You really enjoy phrase-making, don't you?
>
> Sébastien: That's all I have left, my dear. . . .[16]

In Sagan's theater, bons mots, sarcasm, self-deprecating remarks, ironic commentary, or pseudoaxioms are more apt to be responsible for keeping the audience entertained and engaged than chance encounters, mistaken identities, or withheld information. Sagan seems to suggest in this indirect way that words are all that anything is about.

Not only does Sagan privilege dialogue over plot, but she also favors dialogue over stage action, or, rather, the opportunity for stage action. Not for her are the built-in moments of slapstick, revolving-door choreography, or acrobatic gimmicks of a Feydeau or a Courteline, or even the less boisterous stage business of recent Boulevardiers André Roussin, Françoise Dorin, and the duo Barillet and Grédy. Her characters do not, as a general rule, faint, hide, collide with each other or the furniture, fight or dally in parlor games. There are almost never more than four characters on stage at a time and, in most scenes, there are only two—engaged in conversation. Tension rises generally at the point where the exchange becomes confrontational.

Her characters do play cards *(Château en Suède, Bonheur, impair et passe, Un piano dans l'herbe, Le Cheval évanoui),* which permits the actors a certain amount of stage business while they chat. The preponderance of card games also reinforces, perhaps unintentionally, the ever-present Saganian theme of playing at life, as does the serving and imbibing of cocktails that occurs in virtually every play, thus allowing the characters to change personality in mid-Scotch, as it were. Most of her plays contain one dance scene, usually a waltz *(Château en Suède, Les Violons parfois,* and *La Robe mauve de Valentine).* But the music is be-bop in *Un piano dans l'herbe* because the characters are reliving their youth. The dance scene presages, prepares, even stands in for the lovemaking scene that is also present in each play, if always off stage and during a blackout. To be sure, the absent presence of the sex act creates a certain excitement among the characters, but nothing that can be termed "stage action."

In view of this minimal use of physicality and the fairly loose plot of her plays, it should be clear that the theatricality of Sagan's theater work, contrary to the Boulevard model, relies almost without exception on characterization and dialogue. The weaknesses or outright failures of certain of her theater pieces can, in fact, mainly be attributed to a misuse of these two components. Heavy-handed characterization in the beginning of *Les Violons parfois,* for example, presents the characters Charlotte and Antoine as cardboard opportunists, while longwinded revelations at the end of *Il fait beau jour et nuit* bring the play to a close in a fashion more novelistic than dramatic.

On the other hand, when Sagan maintains her light touch and does not resort to melodramatic devices to force a point or establish motivation, she avoids this trap of changing registers. She thus guarantees the continuing impact of the self-conscious humor and whimsy that characterize her best moments and, indeed, her best plays: *Château en Suède* and *Le Cheval évanoui.*

Château en Suède

Seduction and Old Lace. The play begins with sister and brother Eléonore and Sébastien Van Milhem reading together a gothic romance. They are in an isolated Swedish château that belongs to Eléonore's husband Hugo. (All the action takes place in the sitting room of this château.) Their prudish and eccentric sister-in-law Agathe, elaborately dressed, as are Eléonore and Sébastien, in Louis XV costumes, announces the visit of Stockholm cousin Frédéric Falsen.

Hugo, fresh from the fields and not yet accoutered as Agathe's aesthetic taste and the honor of the family dictate, enters in turn. His outdoorsman style contrasts markedly with Sébastien's bored and laconic decadence. Nevertheless, we soon learn from Sébastien, after the brief appearance of a childlike Ophélie, that Hugo also has his faults. He has, for example, sequestered Ophélie (his first wife) and staged her funeral so as to be able to marry Eléonore.

In a family council, Agathe demands that everyone protect the secret of Hugo's outlandish bigamy from the soon-to-arrive Frédéric. She invokes their mother, until then a mass of clothing and blankets hidden in the corner, as gauge of familial integrity. (The apparently paralyzed old woman will remain motionless and speechless until the final moment of the play.) Passing through, as is her wont, Ophélie protests against being locked up again and threatens to marry Frédéric to show Hugo a thing or two.

When the handsome and boyish Frédéric arrives, he shocks Agathe by his modish attire, annoys Hugo, engages in *mondanités* with Sébastien, and falls immediately under the spell of the beauteous Eléonore. Fifteen days later, Frédéric is still recounting his amorous exploits and attempting to impress Eléonore with his hunting prowess: he has killed a teal whose softness he contrasts, in a worn oxymoron, with Eléonore's "freezing hot" nature. In the presence of Sébastien and Agathe, Frédéric wonders aloud about the charming blonde waif he keeps encountering in the halls. Agathe explains that she is a crazed distant cousin. Hugo, about to explode, enters and leaves, while Eléonore warns Frédéric yet again about the imminent snowfall that will entrap him in the château for at least four months if he does not depart soon.

Some time later, Sébastien and Ophélie are playing cards before the fire. Sébastien flirts and Ophélie cheats. Frédéric joins Sébastien, Ophélie having wandered off again, and confides that he loves Eléonore but knows she will make him suffer. He then declares himself to his beloved and Eléonore, unimpressed by his agitation, proposes a rendezvous that night. After having to chase Sébastien and Ophélie from the same trysting spot, Frédéric and Eléonore carry on their adventure. This ends act 1.

Eléonore and Sébastien chat more than amiably about Frédéric's merits as a lover. Sébastien teases her with his own jealousy and then, less amusingly, with the prospects of arousing Hugo's suspicions. Alone with Eléonore, Frédéric complains pitiably about her off-hand treatment. She tells him that he is acting the role of the husband rather than the lover.

Gathered around Hugo, kingly in his arm chair, Ophélie, unwittingly, and Sébastien, on purpose, hint at Eléonore's by now two-week-old liaison. However, Eléonore, in the presence of Frédéric, shows Hugo that he is the only "man" in her life. The snow and its corollaries—Sébastien's taunts, Frédéric's petulance, and Eléonore's paradoxical behavior—are getting on everyone's nerves. Even Ophélie tries to warn Frédéric that he risks great danger from several possible sources, just as she, Hugo's first wife, managed to fall into a trap! Act 2 ends with this revelation of Ophélie's real status enchanting Frédéric.

Eléonore and Sébastien, again alone together on stage, reminisce about their former high-life existence in Paris and jubilate over their present entanglements. Hugo enters the now empty room and hides behind the drapes. While he listens in, Frédéric reveals to the stunned and disapproving siblings (who have returned) that he knows everything about Ophélie and intends to take Eléonore away from Hugo. Emerging from behind the curtain into the again empty room, Hugo throws a tantrum that terminates by his rushing off to plot revenge on Frédéric, with the help of Agathe and their old servant Gunther. Meanwhile, Sébastien and Eléonore worry about the possible genetic connection between themselves and their mad uncle Jan.

The mood changes slightly as the couples Eléonore and Frédéric and Sébastien and Ophélie dance. Sébastien, having drunk too much, cannot stop himself from provoking Frédéric. Unable to listen to any more of his sarcasm, Eléonore throws a few punches at Sébastien. Frédéric runs out to bring back Hugo to settle the quarrel but discovers, instead, that Hugo, in an uncontrollable fury, has just killed Gunther! And thus act 3 ends with the snow continuing to fall.

Two weeks have passed. Now it is Eléonore and Frédéric who are reading the gothic novel. She remarks cuttingly that he has been very nervous of late. Indeed, all the characters seem to conspire to feed Frédéric's panic. But once alone, Eléonore and Sébastien admit that Hugo *is* behaving rather oddly. Sébastien, in particular, is anxious.

While playing two-handed picquet with Hugo, Eléonore again demonstrates her tender attachment. Hugo proclaims that he would not allow her to cheat on him because he would then be obliged to kill her. This would mean that he would find himself, as a result, remarried to Ophélie—perish the thought! Ophélie then declares, in her meandering fashion, that she is pregnant by Sébastien. Whereupon Sébastien takes refuge on the armoire and Hugo threatens to kill the illicit couple. After this, Frédéric tries unsuccessfully to understand Eléonore.

Later, Sébastien and Ophélie scrounge a meal while everyone sleeps. They are forced to hide when Frédéric and Eléonore enter. Frédéric expresses his certainty that Hugo is stalking him! Suddenly, all the lights go out. Hugo bursts in with a shotgun. He discovers Sébastien and Ophélie and locks them in the armoire "for good" where they will surely suffocate. The horrified Frédéric decides to run away and seek help in the village. Once Frédéric has escaped into the snow, however, Hugo immediately releases his captives. All present laugh at Hugo's good joke on them, while Gunther, not dead at all, carries in some wood.

In the last scene—many weeks later and springtime—Agathe and Ophélie knit, Gunther delivers some high-flown lines on the splendid weather, Eléonore and Sébastien wax poetic about their ride in the woods, and Hugo praises the season's abundance of hops. They are all delighted with each other and with the unborn child. After reading the mail, however, Agathe announces disgruntledly that yet another cousin is scheduled to visit. She finds the pattern growing tiresome. To this effect, she reminds everyone of Frédéric's recently discovered bones. With this, they all become dreamy-eyed, contemplating the winter and the cousin to come. Act 4 ends when the old mother, finally reacting, holds up her arms to the heavens in a gesture of exasperation.

Attacking Conventions Through Irreverence and Whimsy. The French expression "building castles in Spain" connotes impossible daydreams. Sagan's "castle in Sweden" not only realizes on stage a far-fetched fantasy but also immediately suggests through her choice of title a parodic disposition. Icy Sweden hardly conjures up the sensual potential of sunny Spain, but, rather, the morbid introspection we have come to expect from the films of Bergman, the plays of Strindberg, or their Norwegian cousin, Ibsen. Sagan, indeed, renders backhanded homage to the two masters of theatrical "realism," as well as to the third celebrated member of the realism triumvirate, Chekhov, by including several allusions to their works in her play: for example, the family's history of madness that haunts both Van Milhems (Ibsen's *Ghosts*), or the teal that Frédéric kills and compares to Eléonore (Chekhov's *The Seagull*, Ibsen's *The Wild Duck*).

Nevertheless, as should be clear by the preceding synopsis of the plot, Sagan's handling of these references has nothing of admiring imitation about it. Neither Uncle Jan nor the downed bird function as a metaphor to help explain the characters' psychological predisposition or to prepare their unrelenting destiny. Rather, Sagan's use of Ibsen and Chekhov, quite like the name of Ophélie (Ophelia of *Hamlet*) that Sébastien has bestowed upon Hugo's first and supposedly dead wife, partakes of the same sort of humor as a mustachioed Mona Lisa—irreverence. It is certainly irreverence that inspired Sagan's dramatic nod to French realist Zola's *Thérèse Raquin*. The Falsen's inoffensive matriarch is a dulled copy of Zola's avenging mother figure, Madame Raquin, who is also confined to a wheelchair and obliged to sit speechless throughout much of the play.

Irreverent and high-spirited in her references to several of Western theater's "giants" of realism, Sagan also takes on nonchalantly a profusion of Boulevard conventions. By deriding the latter through whimsical reversals, she creates a play whose enjoyment resides not only in parody but also in a redefinition of the boundaries of "the inside" and "the outside." In *Château en Suède,* Sagan confuses what is usually rendered undesirable and even unpalatable with what is normally made attractive.

From the first few scenes, it appears that *Château en Suède* is about to develop as a triangular farce in which tension is created through the dangers of adulterous behavior. All the elements of the bedroom vaudeville are present or will be developed: the triangle of husband, wife, and lover; the stage action of propositions, risk-taking, and trysts; the suspense established through suspicion and innuendo. Typical gags proliferate: hiding behind curtains, seeking shelter on (usually in) armoires, confronting the adulterer with mock violence.

However, within a very short time, Sagan throws a motivational monkey wrench into the dramatic working-out of the adultery. Eléonore, the wife, does almost nothing to hide her affair; in fact, as the play skips along, it seems that she wants to be discovered, or, rather, wants her lover to be caught. (Hugo as much as tells Eléonore that he refuses to accuse her.) Frédéric, the lover, does everything in his power to provoke the husband, who would rather not concern himself with what his wife does when he is not at home. When husband Hugo finally does get rid of lover Frédéric, it is because the latter threatens to upset Hugo's bigamous arrangement, not because he is a success at cuckoldry.

Furthermore, the resolution of the conflict contradicts the conventional ending of the bedroom farce. In traditional farce the original couple is reunited while the lover is frequently reintegrated into or reoriented toward a marriage of his own. In *Château en Suède,* the reestablishment of the original married couple Hugo and Eléonore at the end of the play is accomplished through the literal demise of lover Frédéric! In addition, the designation "original married couple" becomes problematic when we take into consideration the fact that there are two original married couples and, overall, three important couples defined at the beginning of this play: the husbands and wives Hugo and Ophélie and Hugo and Eléonore, and brother and sister Sébastien and Eléonore.

A closer glance at the couples, indeed at the triangular configuration

based in the couples, indicates that Sagan has so complicated the givens
of the bedroom intrigue that we might well be advised to think of the
action as a set of simultaneous triangles, much like a three-dimensional
checkerboard. It is immediately apparent that wife Eléonore does not
operate independently. Her brother Sébastien backs up her efforts to
seduce Frédéric, even "doubles" them. At the same time he establishes
himself as the chief rival for Eléonore's affections. (The hints of an
incestuous relationship abound.) Meanwhile, however, Sébastien seduces Ophélie, the other but abandoned wife of Hugo, the discovery
of which leads Hugo to react as "the outraged and jealous mate."

We can sketch, then, five interwoven triangles, if we interpret
loosely the points of "wife," "husband," and "lover." For our purposes,
we might refine our terminology by describing these three positions in
the following fashion: "insider 1" (the object of desire) + "insider 2"
(the possessor) + "outsider" (the character who attempts to replace
"insider 2"). Thus, we have Eléonore + Hugo + Frédéric (the basic
triangle), Eléonore + Hugo + Sébastien (an ongoing tension), as is
Eléonore + Sébastien + Hugo, and also Eléonore + Sébastien +
Frédéric (tense for Frédéric, in any case), and, finally, Ophélie + Hugo
+ Sébastien. There is also, as an additional complication, the barely
suggested but certainly operant triangle of Hugo + Ophélie + Eléonore. With the exception of Frédéric, always on the outside trying to
get in, and Ophélie, who never gets out, being indeed the sequestered
one, the other three characters exist in constantly shifting patterns of
desire. In fact, Eléonore, rather than the pursued, could correctly be
perceived as the pursuer of Frédéric who becomes, then, the object of
desire. This, however, would eliminate the triangular configuration as
outlined above, for Eléonore has no rival to supplant.

One could expect that all this circulation of desire would create such
a highly charged ambience that the snow might melt of its own accord.
Nevertheless, in keeping with the general mood of irreverence, Sagan
even sends up that most fundamental of dramatic (and human) motivations. Desire does not reign, as is usual in a triangular farce. Rather,
playing at desiring governs the action. The only character truly serious
about his passion is Frédéric, the eternal outsider. And as we learn at
the end of the play, though the cycle had been hinted at all along, the
dead Frédéric has merely taken his place among all the other victims
of earnest desire who have been or will be caught in the endless game
at the castle in Sweden.

In this context, the reading of the gothic romance (signaling passion only through aggression), the Louis XV costumes (promising "After me, the deluge"), the vast but unseen palace (distancing the threatening world outside with its labyrinthine struggles), and the snow (protecting and delimiting the playing area) can all be seen as components of a yearly sporting event. Each one contributes a necessary element for the successful completion of the game. And each enhances the pleasure of playing while permitting the insiders to go about their bloody business. A mindscape is thus established on stage which, because contrasted with nothing else and only vaguely compromised by the "normal" nincompoop Frédéric, seduces the public onto a new playground. The gay madness of the Falsen family, which encompasses habitually breaking the number one commandment, appears permissible—permissible, that is, as fantasy.

No character, except Frédéric, offers a sane foil to the others' craziness. Even the noncrazy though addlepated servant, Gunther, begins miraculously spouting precious odes to spring. And Hugo, the "master of the house," the purportedly adult male surrounded by grown-up children, turns out to be the most perversely sociopathic of all. It is he who has masterminded the play within the play within the play, fooling not only Frédéric but also Eléonore and Sébastien, and the audience, too. Among this lot of pleasant zanies, the pedestrian Frédéric looms pathetic. The spectators are as willing to see him disappear as "the gentlemen" of Abby and Martha Brewster, whose poisonous elderberry wine sends their guests "forever after to Panama" in Joseph Kesselring's *Arsenic and Old Lace*.

Kesselring's maiden aunties share the charm of Sébastien and the grace of Eléonore, though they are gracefully charming in a much more ingenuous way. They love each other, too. And they, too, disobey the most stirring commandment without getting caught and without anyone really caring. In both plays, the "inside" which is proffered for the audience's delectation is the opposite of the outside world that Boulevard drama so frequently reflects. In the American farce, however, the naughty sisters are consigned to the crazy bin at the end of the play. And the forthcoming marriage between their uncrazy (because adopted) nephew Mortimer and the girl next door assures the continuation of a saner species.

In *Château en Suède,* the more urbane but the more daffy of the two, the fruit of the family's combined adventure is a baby engendered of their own loony womb. Sébastien's and Ophélie's progeniture, one assumes, will participate in the same altered reality as their parents.

Without so much as blinking an eye—save old Mother Falsen's occasional disapproving gesture—the dwellers in the Swedish asylum will continue cannibalizing the outside world. Yet asylum also means "a sanctuary or place of refuge." In devouring the outside world, Sagan's characters preserve and promote the privileged space of fantasy. Thus Sagan encourages her public to leave the theater still immersed in a batty but invigorating mental Mah-Jongg.

Le Cheval évanoui

A Mid-summer's Knight's Dream.   The play begins in the drawing room of Wembling House, Lord Henry-James and Lady Felicity Chesterfield's estate in Sussex. (All but one tableau will take place in this elegantly appointed Victorian setting.) The Chesterfields are having after-dinner coffee and an acerbic, though witty (thanks to Henry-James) conversation. Henry-James sardonically inquires about the appetite of Bossy, the family's former pet, now stuffed and seated in the corner. He thinks that he and the placid Bossy are good likenesses of one another. The Chesterfields continue to quarrel about their offspring: Bertram, their son, has buried himself in books on Oriental philosophy while Priscilla, their daughter, has found nirvana on the Continent, where she is receiving a final polish before assuming her functions as an eligible young lady of aristocratic British origins.

The problem that organizes the play's development is soon established with the arrival of "Prissy," as the daughter is called. Prissy has returned to the fold with an unexpected French fiancé in tow. Her mother had a more acceptable (and British) match in store for her. However, the beloved, Hubert Darsay, seems to fit Lady Felicity's criteria and she acquiesces to the marriage. Just for good measure, Prissy squeals that she could not live without dear "Hubby." Henry-James, for his part, clearly could not care one way or the other: he thinks his daughter is silly and figures (correctly if noncommitally) that Hubert is a crass adventurer. This is confirmed when Hubert, alone on stage, telephones his girlfriend Coralie in Paris. He urges her to join him in this easy scam by coming over to seduce Prissy's overanxious, defensive, and effete brother Bertram.

When Coralie, posing as Hubert's sister, arrives—hair in a bun, glasses on, and a volume of Heidegger under her arm—Bertram plunges immediately into her snare. Coralie, however, has no intention of taking seriously either the role of enticing intellectual or opportunist and entreats Hubert to forget his latest scheme and go back to Paris with her. Their games have gone on long enough. But Hubert refuses to listen.

Henry-James, on the other hand, suddenly seems to wish to hear everything Coralie has to say, even if he is normally disinterested in the people around him. Back at the house from having ministered to one of his horses who had knocked himself out while jumping, Henry-James goes so far as to flirt openly with Coralie. He remarks that the stunned horse, in his terrible suffering, reminds him of himself. The horse, however, has become more tender through his pain while Henry-James has turned a bit mean. Only Coralie (and the audience) understand after this declaration that the insults Henry-James directs toward his newest guest are really appeals for her attention.

Several days later, Henry-James and Coralie chat on the grass near the estate's tennis courts. Their conversation, riddled with double-entendres, indicates that Henry-James knows everything about Hubert's machinations and his liaison with Coralie. While also teasing her about son Bertram's halting advances, Henry-James allows her again to see his own interest. Coralie is not immune to his flirting. She obviously admires this man who reads *Macbeth* aloud and doctors his emotional fatigue by swathing himself in irony.

Hubert is aware of what is beginning to happen between Coralie and Henry-James. He, too, participates in a veiled verbal sparring match with his host, who turns out to be the stronger opponent. Perhaps this is because Henry-James has had a longer practice of dissimulation and understatement, having, himself, married his wife for her money. Henry-James's example, however, will not dissuade Hubert, nor will Coralie's repeated expressions of disgust at his behavior and her warning that Henry-James, now affectively alone, probably once had a Coralie as well. Meanwhile, as act 1 ends, Prissy, energetically oblivious to everything except her newly discovered libido, wears down "Hubby" in her own way with Olympic-quality tennis, horseback-riding, and lovemaking.

It is the evening of the grand ball Lady Chesterfield is giving in honor of her daughter's and Hubert's engagement. Both Humphrey Darton, a cousin of the Chesterfields, and Bertram Chesterfield propose marriage to Coralie. Humphrey assures her that they will spend their time together delightfully, either water-skiing on the Riviera or having affairs in London. Bertram plans a honeymoon to Tibet where he and Coralie can consult the wise lamas. Such a visit, he asserts, will give their honeymoon some purpose. Henry-James breaks in to save Coralie from the ludicrous courting of the constipated younger generation. He engages in a more sophisticated courtship dance, consisting, in part, of self-deprecation. Coralie stops him short by demanding a kiss.

Hubert, angry at Coralie for showing herself off as sexy and desirable at the ball, acts confused when she tells him that she is leaving Wembling House. She will not stay around to watch his comedy any longer or to encourage Bertram any more. Hubert, nevertheless, still refuses to leave with her. Bertram takes a different tack: because Coralie has decided to go away, he has hysterics in his mother's arms. This makes him, in Henry-James's eyes, almost likable. Henry-James deals with Coralie's decision by carrying some sugar out to the horses.

Thus when the time comes for the chauffeur to drive Coralie to the train station, he finds he cannot start any one of the five Rolls Royces. (Henry-James had fed the sugar to them rather than to his animals.) Coralie realizes this and chooses, since she cannot leave immediately, to stay around until Hubert is married. She will live out the inevitable with Henry-James, the unsuspected automobile saboteur.

Bertram, bereft and most probably witness to his father's and Coralie's splendor in the grass, kicks Bossy into many pieces. His mother is the sole person to lament the shredded friend of the family. For everyone else, and especially for Henry-James, the massacre of Bossy, however momentary, is a liberation.

Bertram then goes on an alcoholic rampage, while Hubert, in an impassioned fury, confronts Coralie with what she has just done. He is shocked to learn that she actually enjoyed making love to Henry-James. Coralie again gives Hubert the choice of leaving with her or of staying on and losing her. But Hubert cannot believe that she will renounce all they have lived together, the way in which he has possessed her, and the eight years of violent emotions they have shared.

In the interim, Bertram has chosen to become an athlete instead of an intellectual, surmising that a muscle man would have a better chance of winning Coralie. His sporting sister Priscilla, taking no pity on the foolish boy, refuses to help him improve his strength and his coordination. This leads to a grammar-school scuffle between the two of them, in which each one reveals the psychological profile of a spoiled six year old.

It is now the day of the marriage and of Coralie's definitive departure. Henry-James wonders, in his bantering way, what she would say if he begged to go with her and if he set about making a new life for both of them, a bohemian existence of love and odd jobs in Paris. Coralie responds that she would have to say "no," for, in spite of everything, she still loves Hubert, even if she plans to erase him from her life.

Understanding her position and her pain, Henry-James then antagonizes Hubert with the fact that he has bought two tickets to Paris for himself and Coralie and that he intends to spend the rest of his life with her. Hubert, really panicked this time, asks Coralie if it is true. Seeing the tickets in Hubert's hands, Coralie finally realizes that Henry-James had been ready to give up everything for her. He loves her. But Hubert, shocked by Henry-James's strategy, loves her too and at last grasps what it would mean to live without her. In a final gesture, Henry-James gallantly gives the two tickets to his rival and sends the reunited lovers away. But before they go, Coralie suggests to "Henry"—as she prefers to call him—that if he had only told her the truth, maybe she would not be going away with Hubert after all. Bemused, Henry-James then calls for some smelling salts for his wife: as act 2 ends, it is clear that Priscilla's wedding to "Hubby" will not take place.

"You Have but Slumber'd Here / While These Visions Did Appear."   If *Château en Suède* is a farce that encourages the public to revel in mischief and regress to irresponsibility, *Le Cheval évanoui* can be characterized as a comedy tinged with pathos. In it the central character, Henry-James, covers up his bitterness and sadness by wit, and the spectators are consequently distanced from his forlorn condition. They are not, however, duped by his cleverness, and, therefore, the "happy ending," or the rejoining of the original lovers, Hubert and Coralie, roars, or maybe only whimpers, with irony. Moreover, not only the character Henry-James but Coralie, too, may be getting the short end of the love stick. Hubert hardly seems any more reliable at the end of the play, despite his protestations of devotion, than throughout the exposition and development.

As in so many of her novels, Sagan in her play *Le Cheval évanoui* shows characters trying to deal with the pressures of living in a world in which "evil" is represented by society (Lady Chesterfield in this case) rather than by chaos or lawlessness. What appears wicked are the responsibilities of adulthood: Henry-James, "the hero," has always refused them. However, although extremely appealing in his refusal, Henry-James is also cut off from his real self and thus closer to the stuffed dog (a scenic metaphor for conformity) and the stunned horse (an allusion to how most people go through life) than to a free and self-directed human being.

The play's repeated references to *Macbeth* embody his impulse to kill the phoney Henry-James so that the other "Henry" can be born, the real one he left behind when he married Felicity, a "Henry" he sees again in his chance to love Coralie. Love, then, as in most of Sagan's plays, represents the only possibility of attaining "the real," yet, it, too, may be an illusion, as Henry-James knows: "You must realize that to be free to be yourself, you have to be free of everything material. And that you must put up with nothing except passion, precisely because passion is not reassuring."[17]

Love certainly establishes a state of extreme fragility, as demonstrated by Hubert's near loss of Coralie. Love also guarantees exquisite pain and confusion, to cite Henry-James again (this time in a paraphrase): "No one says 'my love' anymore because love no longer has a face, because it has had too many faces" (*CE,* 70). But Henry does pronounce the words "my love" one more time and mean them. In the last moments of the play, he and Coralie act out a vignette of life in Paris as it might have been if "Henry's" dream had been allowed to come true. He asks: "What would you like, my love?" She answers: "Whatever you will, my love" (*CE,* 176). Their sketch within the play ends, all the same, and Coralie leaves Henry-James to match her will to Hubert's.

At the close of another, more consequential dream play, Shakespeare's *A Midsummer-Night's Dream,* the character Puck tells the other characters as well as the audience: "You have but slumber'd here / while these visions did appear." Puck's reassuring lines remind us that theater is only fancy, and if its illusions be frightening, they are only so for the duration of the play. Henry-James Chesterfield, the chivalrous knight in Sagan's *Le Cheval évanoui,* on the contrary, lives a life of horror. His beautiful dream provides a unique moment of escape. This Saganian character has the opposite experience of Shakespeare's "Bottom," who has been humiliated by becoming an ass in his dream. It is in life, even if this is "play life," that Henry-James sees himself transformed into horses and dogs. It is in dream, the waking dream of the presence of Coralie Vernet, in which he allows himself to be a man. The smelling salts he has sent up to his wife at the time of Coralie's leave-taking will also reawaken him to the stultifying existence he leads as the "kept master" of Wembling House. In *Le Cheval évanoui,*

Sagan, unlike Puck in *A Midsummer-Night's Dream,* seems to be extolling, as she so often does, the grace state of fantasy as an antidote to life, even if fantasy itself is unenduring.

This recognition, once again bittersweet, is softened, nevertheless, by comic touches ranging from onomastic puns to intrinsically funny character types to chase scenes. In *Le Cheval évanoui* Sagan shelters her audience from the potentially cruel impact of the play's "message' by building a screen of laughter. The names "Henry-James," "Felicity," "Prissy," "Hubby," "Bossy, the dog," and "Joke, the horse" partake of Sagan's amusingly transparent wordplay, transparent, that is, for an Anglophone and, funny, in any case, to a French speaker's ear. While most of the names comment ironically on the conspicuous personality trait of each character, the Christian name "Henry-James" invokes the greatly admired ex-patriot American writer, Henry James. Sagan returns here to the kind of comic irreverence prevalent in *Château en Suède.* In the same vein, she plays on the names of the main characters in Dickens's *Tale of Two Cities* to fashion Hubert's and Humphrey's surnames: D'orsay becoming Darsay and Carton becoming Darton. Even were we not to understand the disrespectful punning, we would probably not miss the rapport between Henry James, writer and Henry-James, character. The former (a longtime resident of both London and Paris) is cherished for, among other things, his wicked portraits of European aristocrats. Henry-James, the character, enjoys ridiculing the gentry as well.

Indeed, with the exceptions of the Henry-James character and Coralie and, to a lesser extent, Hubert, all the other characters are madcap caricatures, burlesqued in speech and stage action. Their infantilism and righteous stupidity liken them to the high-society swells of a Marx Brothers' movie. Like the Marx Brothers' foils, the secondary characters in *Le Cheval évanoui* are insensitive victims of the protagonist's wisecracks and wit. They, also, in the same farcical tradition, engage in stage antics that include brief hysterics, drunken sprees, wild chases, and scenes of hair-pulling and pinching. Furthermore, they are blind to the very obvious shenanigans going on all around them and seem to value or pay more attention to inanimate objects than to human beings. In other words, Sagan creates automatons of Felicity, Prissy, Bertram, and Humphrey Darton. Deprived of their humanness, these characters are choice targets for the public's unself-conscious mirth and for the principal characters' self-conscious cleverness. It is, finally, this

roguish lucidity that differentiates and protects Henry-James and Coralie while making their utopian fancy seem all the more wistful to the
audience.

Relaxing from Reality

Françoise Sagan both laments and shrugs off the labels ideologues
like to place on her: "[I am] always thought of as bourgeois by the
leftists and as a black sheep by the bourgeoisie. Caught between too
chairs. Oh well."[18] It is true that her theater texts have no overt political content and, even while gently satirizing the bourgeoisie, never
really challenge the social order nor address any of the myriad problems
posed by a life without money or position in capitalist society. Her
plays do no consciousness raising of any sort. Nonetheless, as we have
seen, particularly in *Château en Suède* and *Le Cheval évanoui,* her plays
should not, either, be considered, as many Boulevard pieces are, hom-
ages to existing society, nationalistic hymns, or indulgent paeans to
the family. Sagan neither censors sociopathic behavior nor settles on
the necessity of social integration.

Her protagonists, reminiscent of Noël Coward's in many ways, styl-
ize existence to better control it. They emphasize form over content
and tend to see the world as an aesthetic phenomenon. Since Sagan
suspends ordinary "laws of nature" as well as ordinary legal constraints,
her heroes are marvelous, like those of adventure or detective fiction.
Her plays do not provide the comfort of a Neil Simon melodrama in
which "all's well that ends well," but rather inscribe on stage a structureless reality, held together either by manners or by a socially deviant
code of behavior. Like Feydeau, to power her dramatic world Sagan
relies on a kind of zaniness, countering values of order, economy, and
seriousness by stressing play and the imaginary.

Perhaps a reworking of Raymond Williams's insight, which he ap-
plies to all twentieth-century drama, realistic or expressionistic, will
best situate Sagan's theater. Williams sees the same structure of feeling
in all plays that show characters trapped, even if symbolically, in a
room. For him, the four-walled stage represents the mental prison of
late capitalist society, and the frustrated hero stands for capitalism's
inevitable victim.[19] Whether or not one chooses to think of Sagan's
characters as victims of capitalism, it is clear that they refute the concept of "the room as trap." Rather, her characters, if not fomenting
revolt, can be thought of as relaxing from reality. They say thumbs

down to the structures of an environment (and a mind) that other men have created. And they put forth their own, original, and seductive version.

By confusing the patterns of emotional response that are culturally mandated, Sagan's plays, especially *Château en Suède* and *Le Cheval évanoui,* eradicate the distance between a pleasurable absent and an unpleasurable present. They create another dimension of life; that is to say, they realize a liberating fantasy mode. They thus give pleasure not only through their stylization, but also, as Ien Ang points out in her study of soap operas, in what stylization affords.[20] Rather than a flight *into* fantasy, Sagan's plays allow the spectator to play a game *with* fantasy, a game that makes the limits of the fictional and the real more fluid. This constant to and fro of identification and distancing, this imaginary participation in a consciously fictional world, should not be thought of as mere compensation for the everyday. Sagan's escapist drama, a real projection of the imagination, can function as a crucial component of the spectator's psychological health.

We might conclude by suggesting a feminist perspective on *Château en Suède* and *Le Cheval évanoui* that would also account for some of the pleasure afforded in seeing (or reading) Sagan's theater. We speak here of subversive pleasure, to be sure. In both plays, the institution of patriarchy is ridiculed. If Henry-James Chesterfield is the most sympathetic character of the latter play, the designation of "father" or "head of household" has nothing to do with his attractiveness. He is endearing precisely because he refuses these powerful positions. In addition, and again in both plays, the two major female characters, Eléonore and Coralie, while still the locus of desire, as is traditional in all the representational arts, do manage to control their individual situation through adherence to a personal morality. Neither Eléonore nor Coralie is victim to someone else's domination. They stick by their private values, and even if they are not heroic in any conventional sense, they are, in their own way, intrepid.

We cannot, however, ascribe any stronger feminism, feminine vision, or woman's consciousness to Sagan's theater other than what has just been mentioned, particularly because she continues to hold out love as the only promise, albeit dubious, of fulfillment. For the most part, Sagan, like commercial theater artists in general, is locked into a system of representation and a pattern of receptivity that preclude any exploration of the nature of what might be a suppressed woman's language or sensitivity. The compelling silences of Marguerite Duras's characters in *Agatha* (1981) or the construction on stage of how "woman" is fabricated in Hélène Cixous's *Portrait de Dora* (*Portrait of Dora,* 1976), or even the more direct criticism of sexist behavior by the contemporary Boulevard author Loleh Bellon in *De si tendres liens* (Such tender ties, 1984) are out of Sagan's dramatic ken. Her strength as a theater author resides in her manipulation of whimsy, her irreverence, and her frothy wit. The earnestness and seriousness of purpose of her more committed countrywomen would no doubt impinge on her particular dramatic gifts.

Sagan operates best in the extravagant mode which the Irish poet Yeats celebrated. Yeats believed that an altogether reckless theater would alone combat the spectator's moral fatigue. When Sagan's recklessness is tempered by an elegant wit, her theater is joyously capable of recharging the batteries of her public's imagination.

Chapter Five
Fantasies of Revolt and Fantastic Heroines
Moving Away from the Romance

While Sagan's fiction never omits a love interest, the intricacies of the affair, the psychology of the functioning of love, and the centrality of the stages of development, especially the inevitable parting, are downplayed or even missing in certain of her major mode works. In what might be considered a major mode subset, to wit four novels rather reminiscent in tone of the whimsical fantasy found in *Château en Suède*—*Le Chien couchant* (1980),[1] *Le Garde du coeur* (1968),[2] *La Femme fardée* (1981), and *Un orage immobile* (1983)—Sagan even seems to parody other categories of popular fiction. Thus *Le Chien couchant* reads like a pastiched hard-boiled thriller, while *Le Garde du coeur* with its first-person narrator recalls a more urbane style of detective fiction. *La Femme fardée* offers a burlesqued boat adventure and *Un orage immobile,* the least whimsical and a significant departure from the Saganian canon, revives the nineteenth-century confessional novel.[3]

Moreover, Sagan creates quite a different type of fiction in her two volumes of short stories, *Des yeux de soie* (*Silken Eyes,* 1975), and *Musiques de scènes* (*Incidental Music,* 1981). In the first, she chooses to meditate upon death and various forms of dependency. In the second, on the contrary, she sketches strong, even mythic heroines. The latter volume's stories counterbalance the fictions of love addiction basic to her third-person romances.

Sagan's decentered romances, particularly the novels, delight by their playfulness. The author amuses herself and her readers by stretching and exposing the conventions of each popular genre she adapts. For example, in the thriller *Le Chien couchant,* the socially and economically castrated hero Guéret turns into a self-styled Humphrey Bogart after he happens upon a cache of stolen jewelry. The novel punningly suggests that these found "jewels" restore Guéret's manhood.

Sagan's pleasure in pushing conventions to their limits results in overtly implausible and even self-proclaimed escapist fiction, much more so than experienced in her more tightly controlled romances. *La Femme fardée,* a case in point, interweaves the stories of no less than twelve main characters. Flung together on a luxury cruise, they share beds, gambling games, a forgery con, and, crucially, a collective struggle over the face paint of the eponymous heroine. The "good guys" win, freeing in the bargain the painted lady of both her truly villainous husband and the makeup which hides her real self: alluring and sensitive, despite her inordinate wealth. The voyage has at last enabled her to drive off into the Cannes sunset with her forger-lover at her side. Needless to say, he—reformed just as she is—will never have to work again. In another tongue-in-cheek adventure, *Le Garde du coeur,* narrator Dorothy, a Hollywood screenwriter, finally accepts with a light-hearted shrug of the shoulders the lunatic ménage à trois prefigured at the outset. With her new husband Paul, she will look after the sweetly sociopathic and impotent Lewis, a young actor who skillfully and without a second thought kills off anyone who happens to get in Dorothy's way.

These deliberate reversals of what is accepted as real and Sagan's humorous scoffing at normalcy (both lived and literary) can all be understood as fantasies of revolt.[4] In *Le Chien couchant,* for example, Guéret imagines and acts out a newly acquired masculinity. He no longer needs to heed exclusively the self "feminized" by his submissive position in society. His miraculous metamorphosis permits him to acknowledge a different reality. Clarisse, the ex-painted lady of *La Femme fardée,* recaptures control over her own life after years of near catatonic submission to her husband. She declines to live any longer as the ghost of what she might be. And Lewis, "le garde du coeur," by his bizarre commitment to Dorothy, escapes from ever having to perform again as a man. He thus circumvents a task rendered onerous, if not impossible, by his ambiguous sexuality.

The sense of revolt in all these novels—against social background but especially against the limits of masculinity and femininity—is strongest both in Sagan's second volume of short stories, *Musiques de scènes,* and in her novel, *Un orage immobile.* Throughout *Musiques de scènes* emerge victorious portraits of women that counter the dominant image in the third-person romances. In her stories, Sagan paints various characters as "Minerva," "Pasionata," "Amazon," "Avenger," and even "Medusa." These female characters bask in their own glory and tamper with the borders of patriarchy. In the novel, Sagan redoubles the mythic stance. Through a complex narrative shift, she conjoins the masculine narrator Nicholas with the feminine character Marthe, the proletarian heroine of the barricades. Nicolas loses his painfully wrought writing self in contemplation of Marthe's bravura performance against aristocratic privilege. By combining Nicolas's imaginative leap with Marthe's political and sexual revolt, Sagan, in *Un orage immobile,* posits each as a constituent of the same liberating energy.

What follows will concentrate specifically on the problems posed by the narrative voice and complex characterization in this novel as well as on the fantasies bodied forth in five representative stories from *Musiques de scènes.* Both novel and short stories provide antidotal or at least complementary models to the bittersweet vision of the romances. In addition, the feeling of the fantastic that pervades them, as well as the self-consciousness of the first-person narrator in *Un orage immobile,* transport the reader the farthest away from the mimetic or realistic conventions still in operation in most Saganian romances.[5] Sagan creates in *Un orage immobile* and in *Musiques de scènes* what can be termed a "feminine fantastic"—a projection of freedom from all social and sexual constraints. These works express forbidden yearnings, deal in physical impossibilities and inexplicable motivations, and generally attack the patriarchal real. In a different but related vein, this effort culminates in Sagan's 1983 memoirs, *Avec mon meilleur souvenir.*

Musiques de scènes: Variations on the Revenge Fantasy

Profile of the Saganian Short Story. Sagan best sums up her short story technique in a 1972 interview: "Short stories are pirouettes. I always know the beginning and the end."[6] Graceful, coaxing out of the reader a slow smile, even an occasional chuckle, Sagan's stories most often consist of a quick introduction that establishes in a few sentences the main characters, the setting, and the problem, followed by a suspenseful development and a reversal or surprise ending. While this structure calls to mind Maupassant's tales, Sagan, unlike Maupassant, includes no moral lesson nor does she winningly illustrate the peculiarities of a particular social class or milieu. Rather, in her first collection, *Des yeux de soie,* she creates situations in which twentieth-century characters confront their despair and their solitude. The melancholic, sometimes morbid tone of these early stories and their contemporary frame make way in the second set, *Musiques de scènes,* for a triumphant gaiety and a penchant for historical and foreign settings. In *Musiques de scènes,* Sagan skips engagingly from, for example, island immigrants in a 1960s Nice to the world of professional courtesans in early nineteenth-century Naples to Fontleroy Castle in today's England.

These later stories are both broader and more satirical than the pieces in *Des yeux de soie.* They also take as their target the restrictions placed on woman's role in patriarchy. In each of the five stories from *Musiques de scènes* to be analyzed here, Sagan refuses the acceptable female script and imagines for her heroines a gesture not only of revolt but also often one of revenge. Thus her short stories, much like her mystery novels, invent fantasies to compensate for the realities of existence. In them, Sagan proposes mythic figures of the feminine that challenge us to meditate on women's hidden desires, on those aspects of the female psyche sometimes considered to be crazed, and on manifestations of masculinity responsible for the so-called craziness.

"Le Chat et le casino" ("The Cat and the Casino").   It is Saturday afternoon. Angela di Stefano calls her cat Filou who, exceptionally, has slipped away during siesta time. She finds him on the window ledge of her neighbor, the Beauteous Helena. She also finds her husband, dozing peacefully in Helena's equally peaceful arms. Angela is Corsican: voluptuous, fiery, but proud. She therefore walks silently away, stuffing into her purse all the money meant for the latest mortgage payment on their home. As if in a trance, she enters for the first time in her life the shadowy casino on the elegant main boulevard of Nice. There, not quite in control of herself, she proceeds to win 66,000 francs ($10,000), an unhoped for sum of money. As she later sits at a café sipping a drink alone—again for the first time in her life—she imagines everything she can do with her winnings. But she realizes the possibilities mean nothing to her: she loves what she already has. Back at the casino, she signs her victory check over to charity, an act tantamount to a supernatural event in the eyes of the assembled croupiers. Relieved to see her walk in through the door, Giuseppe, waiting at home with the cat on his lap, concedes to himself some guilt over his indiscretion but rationalizes: "From time to time, every man has the right to a little adventure: women just don't understand."[7]

"La Futura."   Leonora Guiliemo, "La Futura," had "for twenty years symbolized pleasure, gambling, debauchery, and other passionate excesses to the gilded Neapolitan aristocracy" (*MS,* 53). Now with

Naples under Austrian rule, she mediates between nobles and occu-
piers. Her countrymen buy what her charms can reap. La Futura regularly carries out schemes to save them from Austrian firing squads.
Indeed, the Count di Palermo, to the euphonious tinkling of a large
pile of golden coins, has just enlisted her help in rescuing his son,
condemned to death for killing a Viennese captain. La Futura responds
by dispatching her dwarfed servant to the countryside to kidnap a replacement for the young aristocrat. When the victim, a bronzed and
rugged peasant, Gabriele Urbino, wakes up from his drugged state in
the presence of La Futura, rather than fight for his life he gives himself
over to any use she wishes to make of him. Disarmed by his submis-
siveness and his beauty, La Futura makes of him the best use she can.
With death hovering nearby, she and Gabriele spend the night in bed,
experiencing passion as never before. Early the next morning in Alexandro di Palermo's prison cell, La Futura watches as her handsome,
generous lover and the haughty, sniveling future count undress and
begin to exchange unbleached linen for silk. She abruptly opts for a
different future for all three, ordering Gabriele to put his own clothes
back on. In this way di Palermo dies "abjectly, sobbing and crying out
that he wasn't himself" (*MS, 62*). Much later in Parma a splendid lady
is spotted strolling on the arm of a tall, blond man. No one, however,
believes that this *bourgeoise* could be La Futura.

"Un an déjà" ("One Year Later").   Justine, abandoned a year
ago by a husband she still loves, feels unsettled and lifeless. She has
learned to play the role of gay divorcée so as not to be forgotten by her
friends. She has cut out a thin, angular, armed woman from "the
roundness that was her past happiness" (*MS, 105*). This evening, in
her friend Judith's home, sitting at the same table, surrounded by the
same people who formed the backdrop for last year's debacle, she waits
for something to happen. For the first time since he announced in the
entryway of Judith's apartment that he was leaving her, her ex-husband
Richard, with his new wife Pascale, is physically present to her, sharing a meal and small talk. Nothing, however, does happen, that is
until Justine decides she has kept up the charade of cheerfulness and
independence long enough. In determining to leave the party before
anyone takes notice, she hesitates outside the entryway where she over-
hears Pascale, in an eerie repetition of the event that changed her own
life, tell a stricken Richard that she no longer loves him: "It's really
over" (*MS, 111*). Justine hurries out the door, bounds down the steps,
acknowledges the spring wind off the Boulevard Saint Germain on her

face and "to her horror and hating herself for it," realizes she "suddenly
feels in top-notch form" (*MS*, 112).

"L'Echange" ("The Exchange").   On this delicate autumn day,
Arthur Scotfield lags behind the other tourists leaving Fontleroy Castle. He intends to steal the small Frantz Hals painting in the upstairs
corridor. Meanwhile, Lord Fontleroy, accompanied by his magnificent
wife Faye—still flourishing at fifty—and her devoted admirer Byron,
sit down to dinner. Lord Fontleroy, always skeptical about Faye's faithfulness, locks her into her private apartments after their meal. Before
smiling good night to her husband, Faye makes a mental note of the
space on the wall where the Hals had recently hung. When she opens
a secondary closet to find a stole that she has not worn for some time,
she finds hiding there also Arthur Scotfield, who quickly, but without
difficulty, invents his adoration: "I had to see you" (*MS*, 150). Faye
had already assessed his potential: "Well-dressed, she thought, he
could be a very handsome boy, despite how thin he is. His eyes and
mouth are superb" (*MS*, 149). After very few preliminaries, Arthur
Scotfield and Faye Fontleroy entangle themselves within each other's
arms. The next morning while Arthur is dressing, Faye calls him back
to the bed to proffer a love note he must not read until on the train en
route to London. He complies, smiling to himself at how effortlessly
he had gotten away with the theft and, also, at how delightful the
night's interlude had been. He keeps on smiling, even after Faye's short
message registers: "Watch out, darling. This painting is about as au-
thentic as your passion for me. (I too need money from time to time.)
The evening was charming. . . . Shall we consider us even" (*MS*, 155)?

"Une question de timing" ("A Question of Timing").   A well-
off Parisian contemplates his ravishing but aloof mistress. While she
embroiders, curled up on the sofa, he thinks about how he has loved
her but also why he must leave her, why he has had to decide to put
her out of his life. She is "fire and ice" (*MS*, 161), completely enigmatic to him, a sensual fury at night, cool as a cucumber during the
day. She has never treated him as an equal and always insisted he carry
out her wishes. And he has performed this farce to the hilt, never
before recognizing her shallowness. He marvels that she does not understand real solitude, that she seems to have never had a childhood,
that she has always been a virgin or perhaps never been one. She is
neither funny nor thoughtful, rather more like a parasite than a human
being. And furthermore, he knows she does not love him and that he
cannot own her. He shivers at his own loneliness. He remembers that

her last lover killed himself two months after she left him, and that she hardly noticed. Then she speaks: "You know, she [says], Cyril . . . loves me, and I'm going to leave you" (*MS,* 171). And fixing on the blond hair whirling about her face, he understands that his world from now on will be hell.

Interpreting Gestures of Revolt and Acts of Revenge.　　In each of the short stories outlined above, Sagan improves upon unsatisfactory reality by creating a female character who prevails over, or in spite of, her situation. These women characters usually refuse to enact what has been determined to be their roles. Or, through recognizing limits, they transcend them. They are self-determined and vigorous individuals on whom the male characters frequently depend. And they live life as they choose, often inspired by a frank and voracious sexuality. In addition, as an alternative solution, they sometimes remain out of their partner's grasp, living their real life beyond the male character's ken. In each story the female character exercises power without renouncing love. Contrary to the message rooted in the third-person romances, love is therefore empowering rather than enervating.

In "Le Chat et le casino," Angela di Stefano at last faces the possibility of choosing by herself the contours of her life. Up until the moment she discovers her husband's infidelity, she had done exactly what had been expected of her—cooking, cleaning, and caring: "for ten years she had done nothing but obey him and try to keep him happy"(*MS,* 11). She has fulfilled her part of the contract, because that is what a woman does.

Sagan creates a situation in which Angela di Stefano embarks on a metaphorical voyage into her self. Out of the blinding sunlight of Nice, she enters as if beckoned into the cool darkness of the gambling hall. There she risks everything, deflecting perhaps what she would have risked had she played out her anger at home. Winning is less important for the security it provides than for the insight it affords into her own potential for power. Her earnings permit her to consider the many paths now open to her and to dwell on the astounding acts of revenge Giuseppe's betrayal elicits. With the reader, she can indulge in fantasies of spectacular exits and vignettes of scornful dismissals. However, she can also identify and put into perspective the various elements of her existence. And she can take responsibility for what her life has been and will be. Rejecting the money permits her to accept her own strength. Indeed, her toughness will compensate for Giuseppe's lack of it. Forever after she can look after her cat and her man

in full understanding of the elaborate frauds of independent masculinity both work so hard to perpetrate.

When Angela di Stefano walks out of the casino the second time,
thereby concluding her inner journey, her sense of worth and dignity
have become unshakable. The ironic tone imparted through Giuseppe's
self-satisfied comments about his own adventure serves to underscore
the far greater adventure Angela has undertaken. She has lived faster,
gone farther, and learned more in one afternoon than Giuseppe probably will in his whole lifetime. Angela di Stefano, a modern Minerva,
has attained wisdom.

In "La Futura," Leonora Guilemo, unlike Angela di Stefano, does
not hold revenge at bay. She both sketches its dimensions and fleshes
them out. La Futura has made high-society Neapolitan men pay for
years for her oppression. As both a member of the lower orders and a
woman, she has exacted their tribute. The Austrian Occupation has
changed none of this. In fact, it has conveniently resulted in an increase
in her powers. The Count di Palermo may complain under his breath
about the "superb but shameless hussy" (*MS*, 54) he believes her to be,
but he is still obliged to seek her aid when his only son becomes the
target of Austrian justice.

La Futura had not met her physical or intellectual match in a man
until the guileless Gabriele Urbino entered her life. And while he remains entirely subordinate to her will, his quiet force and easy joy in
simply existing fuse to end the pattern of destruction her life has taken.
A blue-eyed, fresh-smelling harvest god, Gabriele complements the
divine Futura, who not only has a mythic sobriquet but also a voice
"like a violin" (*MS*, 57) ringing with the music of the spheres. Together they can inhabit a psychic and sexual domain whose existence
is unthinkable to ordinary mortals.

When La Futura sacrifices Alexandro di Palermo in her final act of
retaliation, she not only strikes back at what he represents—a stance
of superiority and the brutality and cowardice superiority fosters—but
she also proclaims her right to a free and unhindered sexuality. All the
world's money will not equalize the puny, repugnant Alexandro and
the beautiful, uncalculating Gabriele. Having lived by sex, La Futura
finally chooses to define her future by it. Nevertheless, she reconsti-
tutes the sex act into a noncommodity, removing it from the realm of
exchange. Embodying the feminine avenger, La Futura will no longer
be bought in any sense.

Justine's revenge in "Un an déjà" takes quite a different form from

La Futura's. More like the character Angela di Stefano, Justine is jolted into grappling with her own possibilities. Her revenge takes the shape of self-awareness. In Justine's case, what does not happen, or rather what happens indirectly to her, provides the pivotal moment. After dwelling so long on her own unhappiness and incompleteness, Justine is cured when this same misery is inflicted on the man who so wounded her.

She too, like Angela di Stefano, goes on an interior voyage, a voyage not represented physically as in "Le Chat et le casino," but one communicated through images of containment. Thus, Justine confronts the real enemy—herself—by staring at her reflection in the mirror of the entryway, by controlling and dissecting her reactions at the dinner table, and, finally, by reliving the original rupture at a distance through the present breakup of Richard's marriage. She escapes from self-pity and pain in a complete emotional reversal as she rushes forth into a new beginning, promised by the spring breeze. Cruelty feels good and revenge is sweet. Justine has not just learned to act like a liberated woman. She is one.

The heroine of "L'Echange," Faye Fontleroy, is made of the same stuff as Doria Doriacci, Sagan's unquenchable diva from the novel *La Femme fardée* and as La Cachionni, an earlier incarnation, the star soprano of the story "La Diva" in *Des yeux de soie*. All three characters stand in opposition to the vanquished Paule of the novel *Aimez-vous Brahms . . . .* These later middle-aged *pasionatas* from Sagan's repertoire love life and men and themselves with equal enthusiasm. Neither their age nor a bourgeois sense of propriety stops them from responding to all sensual urgings. With nary a backward or forward glance, La Doriacci, La Cachionni, and Faye Fontleroy seize every opportunity for a little romance. Yet each operates according to a laudable moral code predicated on not taking oneself so seriously in the awesome pursuit of pleasure that people, especially other women, get hurt.

In "L'Echange," Lady Fontleroy, detecting in Arthur Scotfield a willing object for her momentary attentions, puts aside all concerns not only for stolen property but also for safety. It is as though, in the style of La Futura, her specular enjoyment of a young man informs her instinct for self-preservation. For both these characters, the fountain of youth, personified respectively by Gabriele and Arthur, guarantees the heroine's heady sense of personal value, not merely as a beautiful woman but, more centrally, as a passionate human being committed to squeezing every drop of *jouissance* out of its bearer.

In these fantasies of the aging Amazon, Sagan creates a heroine capable of turning every situation to her advantage. Lord Fontleroy's heavy-handed treatment of Faye proves, then, not just ineffectual but also enabling. His jealous imprisonment permits her to make love to Arthur without worry. Faye avenges herself of Lord Fontleroy's autocratic behavior thanks to the very circumstances meant to punish her. Furthermore, Arthur, her younger, masculine double, diabolically redheaded as is Faye herself, echoes her picaresque, life-affirming qualities. Instead of foreseeing the heroine's defeat as does that other Saganian double, Simon of *Aimez-vous Brahms . . . ,* Arthur partakes of Faye's larcenous freedom, cheerily stolen from a sociosexual structure she participates in only better to undermine.

"Une question de timing" takes place almost wholly in the male character's mind. In this sense, the story parallels "Un an déjà," dominated by Justine's musings. However, whereas in the former story Justine gains a new confidence through overhearing the key phrase, "I don't love you any more" (*MS,* 111), the maudlin "il" of "Une question de timing" receives his mistress's final declaration like a punch in the stomach. "He," rather than empowered by the surprise ending, is undone by it. His mistress deposits him at the gates of hell instead of transporting him to a virtual heaven.

This unknowable woman, understood by "him" only as a kind of sphinx, might be thought of as taking revenge for all the kept women and female objects in Sagan's romances. "She" is neither resigned to financial dependency, as is Lucile in the novel *La Chamade,* nor is she reduced to wallowing in love's abyss, as is Nathalie of *Un peu de soleil dans l'eau froide.* Although the reader has scant access to information about "her," other than the obviously unreliable history constructed by the lover in his attempt to take his distance, two images clamor for examination. Each helps explain her power.

Working calmly on her tapestry throughout this story, like Ulysses's Penelope, "she" seems to wait patiently while "he" determines her fate. This image of Penelope, however, hides the truly analogous Greek heroine lurking just under the surface. With tendrils of hair writhing about her face, the mistress, at the end of the story, more like the rebellious Medusa than the obedient Penelope, forces the lover to come to grips with his impotency and her willpower. Her gaze exerts its full pressure and turns the tables on a concept of woman immured through masculine eyes. The lover, holding to Victorian notions of female passivity, is thus destroyed by his inability to read the Medusan tumult barely contained within an insidious Penelope.

The fantasies of Amazons, avengers, Minervas, Medusas, and *pasionatas* embedded in Sagan's second volume of short stories are not fantasies of the dominant culture, that is, they are not founded on a collective and popularized masculine wish based on self-aggrandizement for the man and self-abasement for the woman.[8] They might, instead, be thought of as representing what women find divine and demonic in themselves. The power of Sagan's women characters to do evil, wreak havoc, or simply enjoy a male character's discomfiture might indeed be seen as a direct function of a perceived women's powerlessness in society to do much else. Sagan's devouring sexual heroines can, then, be understood as battle signs for women's rights to the same sexual freedom as men. Her wise women especially know the laughable arbitrariness of both masculine and feminine roles.

Nevertheless, taken as an ensemble, the short stories of Sagan's second volume, all while positing formidable women characters, do almost nothing to counter society's reigning male-female polarity. They merely inverse the givens, maintaining different spheres and permitting women characters the privileges hitherto restricted in Sagan's prose fiction to the men.[9] In her novel *Un orage immobile,* however, Sagan moves beyond the powerhouse females of *Musiques de scènes* to invent a composite hero/ine. In the 1983 work, she imagines a doubled principal character—male and female—who takes revenge on a patriarchal mentality by transfiguring sex not only into a rifle but also into a pen.

Un orage immobile: The Woman's/The Writer's Revolt

Profile of *Un orage immobile*.   From its opening paragraphs, *Un orage immobile* proclaims its uniqueness from all other novels of the Saganian canon. Her trademark beginning, a charming but somewhat detached establishing of an emotion, usually filtered through natural images—for example, sadness via silk in *Bonjour Tristesse,* expectation via a sunset in *La Femme fardée*—is here replaced by the first-person narrator's direct apologia à la Rousseau. His claim of writing only to put to rest the horror of the story he is about to tell succeeds in binding the reader to the narrative with a kind of ghoulish anticipation. Rather than providing the emotional rolling carpet effect of the debuts of most of her other novels, *Un orage immobile* plunges us immediately into the concerns of the narrator as writer, foregrounding the experience of turning life into literature. In this respect, the novel reminds us of Sagan's semiautobiographical fiction, *Des bleus à l'âme.*

This is not to say that the romantic fallacy is inoperable. In fact, Sagan offers here her lushest descriptions: the first-person narrator invests more time than any of her others in suggesting correspondences between his own situation and the surrounding countryside. For instance, as a young man absorbed by the turmoil of sexual initiation, he can only focus on the (feminine) fields outside his windows overpowered by the (masculine) sky: "a plain where the Sky stretches itself out endlessly, where the small rose-colored and white clouds—those round and gamboling clouds—blue and bright red in the Western sunset, cannot disguise nor diminish the gesture of possession the sky has always had towards our lands."[10]

The ourpouring of the narrator's sensual feelings makes this the most romantic of Sagan's novels. In *Un orage immobile,* Sagan consciously parodies a late–eighteenth-century/early–nineteenth-century *roman personnel.* Techniques of direct address to the reader, preciousness in tone, and archaic expressions bespeak the desire to imitate romantic models. Nevertheless, the historical setting (the novel takes place between 1832 and 1862) and the love story that takes place within it (between the aristocratic Flora de Margelasse and the peasant Gildas Caussinade), as well as sundry other romantic trappings, merely serve as a scaffolding on which Sagan hangs a more complicated fantasy of liberation.

In *Un orage immobile,* Sagan conjures up and combines a fantasy of creative revolt, embodied by the narrator Nicolas, with a fantasy of political and sexual revolt, expressed through the character Marthe. In the last third of the novel, the introspective first-person narrator stops thinking about himself in order to devote his full attention to the fantastic Marthe whose fate, rather than his own, closes the novel. The center of interest is thus displaced from Nicolas-narrator, contemplating his writing and re-creating the core event of his life, to Marthe-character. Through the process of reading, these two figures merge into one. It then becomes possible to comprehend *Un orage immobile* as the revolt of the woman writer—split, layered, and fragmented—like the pieces of Humpty-Dumpty, but capable through reading of being put back together again.

The Still Storm Erupts.[11]   The narrator, an old man named Nicolas Lomont, after excusing himself for the literary flashback he is about to perform, takes us to the summer of 1832 in Aquitaine, specifically to the city of Angoulême. He is just beginning his career as *notaire,* a highly respected position that joins the duties of lawyer to those of accountant and notary public. He will recount, it appears, the story of his sexual awakening. However, in his initial description of himself his emphasis on his delicate hands and long fingers already hints at what will eclipse the story of emergent manhood, that is, the story of emergent writer. From a recorder of facts, statistics, and numbers, Nicolas, by composing this narrative, is changing himself into a creator: "What else of such importance is left to me but to gaze at my hand, still fine, but now with veins thrusting outwards like securing ropes, my hand engaged in adding one small blue sign to another. . . . I have never experienced this feeling in drawing up any legal or actuarial document: there must be something to this, after all—a magical childhood given back to writers when they write" (*OI,* 14–15).

He proceeds to tell the story of Flora de Margelasse and Gildas Caussinade, adding along the way his own part in the tragic affair. The young widow, Lady Flora Knight, née Margelasse, born in exile after the French Revolution, returns to her family's estate to take up life again in Aquitaine. Nicolas, summoned to her home to conduct her affairs, falls immediately in love with her. He is, nonetheless, too timid to tell her so. Flora's grace, energy, and beauty win over all of Angoumois society, including the acknowledged social queen, Artémise d'Aubec, the prefect's wife.

Nicolas spends nearly a year and a half picnicking, riding, dancing at Flora's side, and advising her on business matters. He remains entranced, while nevertheless noting how she gently sidesteps any romantic confrontation. However, when the dark and handsome Gildas Caussinade, a local tenant farmer's son and promising poet, is introduced to their world, Nicolas sees that Flora can respond with more than polite interest or even friendly warmth. She willingly accompanies Gildas to the d'Aubec's balcony—that threshold so dear to romantics—and shares there the tension borne of awakening desire.

Although the Aquitainian dignitaries fete Gildas for the glory he brings to their part of France, they will not consider him one of their own. Flora, on the contrary, refuses to confer importance on the social gulf that separates them. She and Gildas give in, without any caution, to their mutual attraction. In the midst of the scandal provoked by their love affair, Flora and Gildas depart for Paris. There, Gildas, sponsored by Alfred de Vigny and friends, swells the ranks of the young lions of romanticism. Moreover, in recognition of his poetic and dramatic works, the king ennobles him.

Two years later, Flora and Gildas return to Angoulême where they reconquer the admiration of the gentry. They become the center of a turbulent social whirl, strangely colored by the mysterious presence of Marthe, a servant they have brought back from Paris. All the noblemen of the region grow figuratively, if not literally, ill from a compulsion to possess this fearsome creature. Gildas, himself, does not resist her spell.

Aware of the emotional chasm awaiting Flora should she learn of Gildas's unholy attachment, Nicolas despairs of controlling this other, darker woman who seems to have no price. Marthe herself is curiously complicitous with the very disturbed Nicolas. She saves his life during a ludicrous duel in which he seconds Gildas's honor. She also, however, provokes the suicide of the prefect, Honoré d'Aubec, and, later, of a schizophrenic Gildas. On the day of her wedding to Gildas, Flora lurches into insanity when she learns that he has already secretly married Marthe. Gildas kills himself shortly thereafter. Many years of futile searching lead Nicolas to at last track down Marthe on the Parisian barricades of 1848. It is too late to award her the vast fortunes left her by a series of thwarted lovers. In the service of an unending revolution, Marthe has received a bullet in the heart.

The "I" of the Storm.   Like the "I" of *Bonjour Tristesse,* the first-person narrator of *Un orage immobile* possesses several dimensions, more, in fact, than can be characterized by such terms as the "Experienced I" and the "Acting I," although these expressions do help clarify Sagan's earlier voicing technique (see chapter 2). Here the "I" is composed not only of the embittered old man telling the story and the naive young one whose story he tells, as well as introspective components of each, but also of a more distanced, omniscient "I," who knows more than he should to be classified as a first-person witness or confessional narrator. The latter conveys, for example, details about Flora's past in England to which even "Nicolas, the admiring friend," would never have been privy.

Moreover, Nicolas-narrator evidences two distinct approaches to the story, or rather stories, he tells. He wavers between the "recorder Nicolas" and the "creator Nicolas," with the former structuring the narrative through dates, claiming to reconstruct the past from notes jotted down in his daily calendars of the period, and the latter unfolding lyrical meditations that tend to overwhelm the cramped and angry voice of the recorder. The "creator Nicolas," palpably thriving on the play of language that permits him, for example, to juggle three possible designations for "house"—"château," "batisse," and "demeure" (*OI,* 15),—is very attractive to the reader. Equally attractive is the "young Nicolas," whose perspicacity vis-à-vis his own emotions communicates several exquisite affective moments. The "aged Nicolas," on the other hand, as well as the "recorder Nicolas," because, respectively, of their self-involvement and repressive, orderly style, distance the reader's affections. Thus the prismatic first-person voice establishes an intricate and challenging rapport with the reader, a rapport, nonetheless, eased in the last third of the novel when the "creator Nicolas" comes to the fore and the fantastic cast of the tale he tells veils any suggestion that the narrative re-creates "reality."

Attempting to ascertain just who *is* this Nicolas-narrator is further complicated by the presence of other characters who, rather than highlighting his specificity, seem to obscure his boundaries. Sagan's romances, in the main, develop important distinctions between the lovers. In *Un orage immobile,* however, despite superficial differences inspired no doubt by the desire to conform to romantic stereotypes— thus Flora's golden locks and Marthe's jet-black hair—her characters replicate each other. Flora—robust, healthy, noble, and kind—mimics Nicolas's moral stance. Gildas lives the same solitude, fears the same empty bed as his rival. He too suffers the pangs of literary creation. All three, each in his or her own way, revolt against the social structures that would define their place in the world. And all three continue to like each other, even though they pose momentous threats to one another's peace of mind.

In addition, *Un orage immobile* indiscriminately attributes features of masculinity and femininity to both male and female characters. In his insightful review of the novel, Bertrand Poirot-Delpech praises especially the undetermined sexuality of the narrator. He offers his own curious attraction to Nicolas as proof.[12] Nicolas has indeed many commonly accepted feminine traits. He backs away silently from the scene that wrecks his happiness. He martyrs himself for love. Flora, also sharing masculine and feminine characteristics, boasts "a silhouette more boyish than feminine" (*OI,* 29) and drives her horses with a sure and masterly hand. Even the markedly masculine Gildas proves a terrifying victim of love addiction, a sickness usually reserved for women, but here present in all three characters.

By far the most astonishing symbiosis occurs between narrator Nicolas and character Marthe. Nothing prepares us for the mutual sympathy that grows between them. Even before Nicolas walks in on an odious scene of cunnilingus between Gildas and Marthe, he sees her as an incarnation of untamed female bestiality, a succubus inhaling the

aristocracy into her dim hole, an "Old Crone" (*OI*, 149) towing death
in her wake. He tries repeatedly to encourage, persuade, or threaten
her to leave Angoulême, to abandon what amounts to a campaign
against its menfolk who are "scarred to the bone, on their wrists and
their necks, by burning memories" of her (*OI*, 161).

Yet he, too, is caught up in Marthe's fire. Consumed by thoughts
of her, as are all men who have come in contact with her lubricious
smile, Nicolas begins to daydream of visiting a Bordelais prostitute
who will look just like her. His fascination with her—particularly as
subject of his narration—even replaces his ruminations about the act
of writing, ruminations that account for the most compelling digressions in the first half of the book. Nicolas-narrator eventually disap-
pears behind Marthe's story.

Nonetheless, Nicolas, if succumbing to the desire to tell her story,
does not immolate himself on the altar of her sexuality. Alone of all
her admirers, he appreciates Marthe as not merely corporealizing death
but also, and more meaningfully, defeating it. On the night of the last
fateful masquerade ball, with every character in attendance, Nicolas
listens in on her orgasmic scream. While reeling from the sound, he
also experiences something—perhaps the force of life itself—that he
has never experienced before. As if in recognition of this vicarious com-
munion, Marthe and Nicolas later come together on the dance floor in
a shared and startling burst of laughter. This miracle of complicity
continues when Marthe, for no apparent reason, saves Nicolas's life in
a duel early the next morning by distracting with lascivious whisper-
ings his opponent, a champion marksman.

To elucidate the Nicolas-Marthe connection, we might turn to a
consideration of the violent storm that erupts on the elegant Place
d'Armes after Honoré d'Aubec confesses his hopeless passion for
Marthe. Nicolas glances out the window: "The sun disappeared all of
a sudden. . . . There I saw, scattered over the Place d'Armes and flying
about everywhere, not only newspapers or the usual fallen leaves, but
also unbelievable filth, doubtlessly blown in from the outlying dis-
tricts, shreds of glass, cork, and finery, incongruous bits of garbage
unknown to this spot and these people. There was something sinister
in this show of misery flung into our bourgeois decor" (*OI*, 167). Nicolas has listened to Honoré and been appalled. But at this point in
the narrative, he has also had to admit his own frustration and even
rage.

The tempest he describes does not, then, merely symbolize Marthe's effect upon the community. It also gives form to his own pent-up fury. From this passage to the end of the novel, it becomes increasingly clear that Marthe, by her destructiveness in Angoulême and, after that, throughout the whole of France, will accomplish what Nicolas, a closet revolutionary, can only imagine. Indeed, as he begins to evoke her acts of terrorism, narrator Nicolas stops speaking of his writing as painful. An alter ego, Marthe erupts in life when Nicolas can only revolt through the act of writing. But even Marthe uses words to kill. She forces Honoré and Gildas to write love letters to her, then confuses on purpose their contents as she mockingly recites them back to each lover.

To delve more profoundly into the link between Nicolas and Marthe, we might even posit that the two, along with Gildas and Flora, are facets of the same mind. As in *Des bleus à l'âme,* the incessant return to the writer's concerns with creativity, especially in the first part of the novel, indicates how the characters spring from the writer's consciousness. Their similarities, as seen above, help confirm their common origin. We might think of the characters, then, including the various renditions of Nicolas, as suiting the narrator's fantasies of himself. He, the "still storm" of the title, blows apart in the act of writing.

The temptation is also great to imagine "F. S.," the authorial persona of *Des bleus à l'âme,* transmogrified here. Even if physically absent from the narrative, we can intuit her as the novel's ultimate reference through the incidences of inter-, or rather, intratextuality. More frequently than in any other of her novels, Sagan, in *Un orage immobile,* instead of depending on the classical (and patriarchal) canon, refers back to her own works as inspiration, source, and authority. The book's title comes from her previous novel, *Le Lit défait,* where it is cited as the title of a work by playwright Edouard Maligrasse. Maligrasse, "author of *Un orage immobile,*" lends his name in near-perfect anagrammatic form to Flora de Margelasse. In *Le Lit défait,* as in *Un orage immobile,* the narrator also divides his loyalties between characters. *Le Lit défait*'s narrator sympathizes with the positions of both actress Béatrice and writer Edouard.

Just as Sagan hints with the anagram Maligrasse-Margelasse at how authors hide themselves in their characters, just as she shows how a writer can identify equally well with two characters, we can surmise how she embeds herself, or at least her persona, "F. S," in the characters of *Un orage immobile.* Nicolas Lomont can thus be seen as a not quite satisfactory representation of the artist. Like many other woman writ-

ers, Sagan, in Nicolas, creates a male character to do what she does in
real life—write and think about writing. But she also proposes a female
character who explodes in apparently inexplicable acts of demolition.
Might not Marthe, then, be more than the double of a submissive and
good Nicolas, or for that matter of a passive and willing Flora? Perhaps
she should also be understood as the materialization of the fantastic
dream of escape of a female consciousness imprisoned in a male
narrator.

The Feminine Fantastic: Writing is the Best Revenge

It is possible to sense some dissatisfaction in Sagan's tendency to
parody traditional narrative modes. Her self-consciousness in these endeavors clearly suggests that she is aware of producing an imitation of
order. In her parodies, and especially in *Un orage immobile*, a certain
uneasiness surfaces. These works do not quite hold together in a conventional way, but rather seem to change focus.[13] It is as if Sagan struggles with a form that does not really allow her to say what she wants
or needs to say. And so she subverts her own work, or at least mars its
patina, by producing not just an imitation of order but—and this is
far more tantalizing—a fairly clumsy imitation of order. This discon-
tinuity has allowed us in *Un orage immobile* to both locate the narrator's
anger and infer the author's.

In the short stories of *Musiques de scènes,* anger in the shape of fantasies of revenge and dreams of revolt is less layered and less guarded.
Sagan's stories do not prompt us to speak of the hidden strategies of
the weak. By brandishing heroines who rise above patriarchal limits as
well as defamiliarizing and destabilizing the everyday, the author urges
a consideration of patriarchy's implications. The heroines in her short
stories disdain a sexual exchange in which women are the objects of
circulation. They avenge themselves on a society which functions according to a system of masculine domination. On one of the levels on
which it can be read, *Un orage immobile* can also be seen as providing
an extreme example of this behavior. Marthe, in destroying Gildas,
destroys the embodiment of the perfect Western male—physically
magnificent and intellectually gifted.

Marthe and the mythic heroines of Sagan's short stories are, then, a
far cry from what Nancy Miller has uncovered as the female tradition
in French letters, that is, "heroines who transcend the perils of plot"
by proving to be better than their victimizers.[14] In Miller's scheme,

French women authors' heroines, beginning with la Princesse de Clèves, bypass their erotic longings. They conquer a sense of worth through self-denial and a self-exalting dignity, even if ending up maimed, dead, or in a convent.

Sagan's fantasies, however, do partake of what Miller terms, in the same tradition, the implausible, or comportment which is not quite understandable in terms of either the fiction or a logic relying on cultural conventions. Miller calls these conventions "maxims" or perceptions of "how things are": they replace notions of cause and effect. No maxim, for example, accounts for Faye Fontleroy's sly exploitation of Arthur Scotfield or Marthe's empathy for Nicolas. "How things are" does not explain or condone any of her heroines' acts of revenge. Rather, the revenge takes on the contours of settling scores not even perceived by the male characters (let alone most men and women in society).

Furthermore, as noted in our discussion of *Un orage immobile,* the revolt is more than that of a power-hungry female figure. The narrator-writer also cuts loose. Coming to grips with the anger Marthe incarnates gives Nicolas his tongue. What he represses or contains finds an outlet in his text. We have suggested that this is true of the author Sagan as well. Anxiety of authorship may again have encouraged her to masculinize her fictional author. But there is ample evidence in *Un orage immobile* that he is merely a blind for a feminine—or better, feminist—consciousness.[15] We might compare the creation of Nicolas to the way Sagan in life, in a complementary fashion, constructs herself as "female" by paying such close attention to clothes. Her general performance mode may really have to do with her difficulties in being a "woman," just as Noël Coward's posing, which we have compared to her own, had to do, according to John Lahr, with his disquiet about being homosexual.[16]

Since most writers are men, since the writer is normally constituted as "male," it is not surprising that Sagan's desire to be taken seriously leads her in her fiction to create male authors. She cedes to this same temptation, if not necessity, in her 1983 memoirs in the chapter on her writer's pedigree. There, she cites only literary fathers, even though, as discussed earlier, the major intertextual reference in her third-person romances is to Colette, a literary mother, and in *Un orage immobile* (which for a change boasts no epigraph) to herself. If, in fact, as she repeatedly claims, Proust is the author who has most haunted her, it may well be the problem of identity formation, of the fragmented self fundamental to his *recherche* that strikes the responsive chord. We can understand more significantly this fragmentation as typical of the woman who would also choose to be a writer.

Italo Calvino's idea that the "I" who writes is always a mask, whether the "I" be a fictive or an autobiographical one,[17] leads us, in the guise of a conclusion, to muse on the connection between the "I" of *Un orage immobile* and the "I-memorialist" of *Avec mon meilleur souvenir.* In the former, the splintered "I," as well as the composite hero/ine we have sketched, allows the author to luxuriate in a full-blown fantasy that rejects the realistic screen found in most of her romances. In her memoirs, which immediately follow the novel, she continues to bask in the pleasure of legendary re-creation. Here, however, she fashions the self she wishes to be as though there were no fantasy in her re-membrances. Nevertheless, the outsized portraits of *Avec mon meilleur souvenir* solicit a reading of the autobiography as an ongoing fiction. It behooves us here to recall again that she has chosen to write under the name of "Sagan," the family name of several of Proust's most refined characters. Her pseudonym teases us with the possibility of her own persona's "fictivity."[18] Like Calvino, and like narrator Nicolas, Sagan seems to acknowledge that creating—a fictional or an autobiographical "I," not to mention a third-person narrator—always accomplishes an act of imaginative freedom, a process of revolt (even if only virtual) against the many different prisons that hem us in. As a woman and a writer Sagan's best revenge may well be the "I" who emerges from the memoirs—an ironic daredevil, uncontained and uncontainable in any cliché of the feminine or the female, and fully in command not only of her life but also of her words.

Chapter Six

Sagan Within a Literary "Sorority"

Françoise Sagan shares with other French women writers of popular fiction, notably Christiane Rochefort, Françoise Mallet-Joris, Geneviève Dormann, Régine Deforges, and Marie Cardinal,[1] certain characteristics that reflect the barely nascent feminism of their generation. Coming to writing in the 1950s or early 1960s, before a vigorous women's movement began reorienting literary praxis, they nevertheless chose to write novels with female questers at their center. The heroine's search for a separate identity provides their novels' focus while her introspection usually informs the narrative voice.

This group of writers in no way constitutes a school or even a movement. Each one in her own fashion adheres to what is commonly accepted as "good literature," that is, well-written narratives with sustained plots; stories that refuse to indulge in prurient or voyeuristic sexual interests. Yet together their works, from Rochefort's satires of consumerism to Cardinal's psychoanalytical explorations, effectively and creatively speak the common wisdom of their time—wisdom that should be understood as an awakening to the fetters of gender.[2]

Thus like Sagan, Rochefort, Mallet-Joris, Dormann, Deforges, and Cardinal basically compose love stories, the only kind of story, according to Joanna Russ, which in our culture has allowed for the emergence of a female protagonist.[3] Within the framework of their romantic adventures, the heroines strive to break free of sexual and social conditioning. In Mallet-Joris's *Le Rempart des béguines (The Illusionist,* 1951), for example, a novel frequently compared to Sagan's *Bonjour Tristesse* because of its teenaged narrator and supposed immorality, the heroine Hélène liberates herself from a stifling bourgeois upbringing through an affair with her father's mannish mistress. In Dormann's *Je t'apporterai des orages* (I'll bring you stormy weather, 1971), José, the main character and wife of an influential banker, finds her true but almost inexplicable self in an adulterous liaison with a gangster.

Masochism, madness, or martyrdom do at times win out over the determined and idiosyncratic heroines' attempts to establish a space of their own. The character Maria, for example, suffers an emotional collapse in Cardinal's *Ecoutez la mer* (Listen to the sea, 1962), while Josyane of Rochefort's *Les Petits enfants du siècle* (*Children of Heaven*, 1962) slips unawares into the same morass from which she has tried ineffectually to escape. The barriers to each heroine's success, if not always clear to her are, nonetheless, almost always transparent to the reader. Rochefort's irony, for example, alerts us early on to the politics of poverty and gender that destine Josyane to the same spiritual void as her mother. These novels, then, like many of Sagan's, can serve as warnings about women's entrapment within a patriarchal mentality.

Just as Sagan does, Mallet-Joris, Cardinal, Dormann, Deforges, and Rochefort offer, in the main, what might be termed a cushioned revolt. If through valorizing the inner life of their heroines they reject sexist notions about women's passive nature, these authors also temper any overt hostility toward patriarchy. Some, like Cardinal in *Les Mots pour le dire* (*The Words to Say It*, 1975), hint at coping strategies. Deforges, in her three-volume social melodrama of the Occupation, *La Bicyclette bleue* (*The Blue Bicycle*, 1981–85)—despite her remarkably independent and audacious heroine—goes so far as to stress regeneration through romantic love. However, although these writers affirm the primacy of the male-female bond, they deny the myth of male superiority. In Cardinal's *Les Mots pour le dire*—a case in point—the heroine, with no help from any man in her family, regains her sanity after a harrowing inner voyage.

This group of authors also refuses the supremacy of the institutions of marriage and the family. Rochefort, for one, in *Les Petits enfants du siècle,* cuttingly demonstrates how the concepts of such institutions undermine any chance for real self-determination. As a complementary strategy, several authors remain, as does Dormann in *Je t'apporterai des orages,* morally ambiguous about the sovereignty of the male-female tie and cynical about its durability. Through their fiction all these writers proclaim the sexual emancipation of women.[4] Their heroines, albeit to a lesser extent than the viripotent Léa of *La Bicyclette bleue,* experience sexuality as enabling. Accepting their sexual selves facilitates the formation of their private subjectivity. The sex act does not become just a means by which they perceive themselves as "other"—a self in relation to a male.

Sagan's uniqueness within this sorority of protofeminists rests with her lightness of touch, itself manifested in the pleasurable fantasies she constructs and the lilting tone she maintains. None of the other writers discussed weaves her stories with the same balance of tenderness and wit. Mallet-Joris's prose is certainly as measured as Sagan's, but it is also often ponderous. Neither she nor Cardinal, with her wounded heroines, elicits much laughter, let alone an occasional smile. To be sure, Deforges, in *La Bicyclette bleue,* sweeps the reader away in her exploit-laden panorama of World War II. Her lovers appeal exactly as do Scarlett O'Hara and Rhett Butler, prototypes to which they owe their passion and their wiles. However, Deforges, more than any of the contemporaries mentioned here and far more than Sagan, spends her energy on the intricacies of plotting. Her fiction never approaches the stylistic panache of Sagan's.

Dormann—perhaps the quirkiest, surely the most versatile writer— comes closest to Sagan's particular charm. She combines dream play, interior monologue, and lyrical description in a much richer mixture than found in Sagan's prose. In her fictional world the commonplace assumes a magical aura. Like Sagan, Dormann forsakes detailed analysis for suggestivity. Unlike her, she willingly loses control, challenging the reader's ability to believe. Also in contrast to Sagan, she masters the colloquial verve practiced with even more enthusiasm by Rochefort. She does not, however, nor does Sagan, possess Rochefort's penchant for excoriating comedy.

Among these contemporaries, Sagan's endearing "peculiarity," as John Weightman puts it, is a display of genuine sentiment played out "on the dangerous edges of life, where sentiment can flirt with disaster."[5] With assured writing and sure entertainment, Sagan meets the vast public where it no longer fears to tread. And within this space, she inscribes—if her reader chooses to hear it—the murmurings of a new consciousness.

Notes and References

Preface

1. "Le nouveau Sagan est arrivé" was reported in a June 1969 unattributed article on *Un peu de soleil dans l'eau froide,* consulted in the dossiers of the publishing house Flammarion (March 1985).

2. Bertrand Poirot-Delpech, *Bonjour Sagan* (Paris: Herscher, 1985), 5.

3. It is interesting, however, to note how the official Soviet critics understand Sagan's immense popularity in the Soviet Union. They read her as they do Balzac—as a writer whose novels patently demonstrate the flaws in the capitalist system.

4. An outstanding exception to this dearth of solidly grounded and revisionary studies in Marian St. Onge's Ph.D. dissertation, "Narrative Strategies and the Quest for Identity in the French Female Novel of Adolescence: Studies in Duras, Mallet-Joris, Sagan, and Rochefort," Boston College, 1984, University Microfilms International, microfilm DEQ84–15617. A new biography of Sagan by Jean-Claude Lamy (*Sagan,* Paris: Mercure de France) to appear in 1988 is based on in-depth interviews with Sagan herself as well as her friends, family, and colleagues. Mr. Lamy has indicated (personal communication, November 1987) that he includes sociological insights as well as a detailed study of the publication of *Bonjour Tristesse.*

5. Hélène Cantarella, *New Leader,* May 1955.

Chapter One

1. *Avec mon meilleur souvenir* (Paris, 1983), 85–86; hereafter cited in the text as *S.*

2. Unless otherwise noted, the information in this chapter comes from Sagan's three autobiographical texts: *Toxique* (Paris, 1964), *Des bleus à l'âme* (Paris, 1972), and *Avec mon meilleur souvenir* (Paris, 1983) as well as from some eighty interviews collected in *Réponses* (Paris, 1974) and hundreds of press clippings and articles consulted in the files of Julliard, J.-J. Pauvert, Flammarion, Gallimard, E. P. Dutton, and the Bibliothèque de l'Arsenal.

3. For example, before Sagan married Guy Schoeller, a man old enough to be her father, she published *Un certain sourire* (Paris, 1956) in which the teenaged protagonist has an affair with a man in his fifties. While dating American painter Bob Westhoff, whom she was soon to marry, she published *Des merveilleux nuages* (Paris, 1961) in which the anxious young heroine is married to a neurotic, independently wealthy American artist.

4. François Mauriac, *Le Figaro,* 6 June 1954.

5. Gérard Mourgue in *Françoise Sagan* (Paris: Editions Universitaires, 1958), 18, reports that *Bonjour Tristesse* generated precisely eleven kilos and four hundred grams of newspaper clippings.

6. The publicity director of E. P. Dutton, Elliott Graham, who was in charge of organizing Sagan's first trip to the United States, has collected three scrapbooks of press clippings on this voyage. His records show that after its publication in English in February 1955, *Bonjour Tristesse* remained on the best-seller lists for some twenty-five weeks. The *New York Times Book Review* of 5 June 1955 cites *Bonjour Tristesse* as one of the three best-selling books of 1955.

7. Marcelle Auclair, *Marie-Claire*, 12 May 1956.

8. Jean Lignière in *Françoise Sagan et le succès* (Paris: Edition du Scorpion, 1957), worried by the phenomenal success of *Bonjour Tristesse*, explains in a polemic its unconscious celebration of both the "Eternal Feminine" and lesbianism.

9. Georges Hourdin, *Le Cas Françoise Sagan* (Paris: Editions du Cerf, 1958), reads her first novels as cries for help and urges her back to Catholicism.

10. Mourgue in *Françoise Sagan* speaks of her perfect amorality and faithfulness to a self untrammeled by social constraints.

11. Patrick Poivre d'Arvor, *Journal de dimanche*, 18 March 1984.

12. In 1984, Sagan, along with Mariel Hemingway, Donald Sutherland, Guy Laroche, and several others, won one of the ten best-dressed awards of the Metropolitan Club of New York. In addition, from the first appearance in 1984 of the French fashion magazine *Femme*, edited by her friend Peggy Roche, Sagan has regularly contributed articles on style and stylish people.

13. Bertrand Poirot-Delpech, *Bonjour Sagan* (Paris: Herscher, 1985).

14. Jean-Louis Echine, *Nouvelles littéraires*, 7 April 1977.

15. *Réponses 1954–1974* (Paris: 1974); hereafter cited in the text as *R*.

16. *Des bleus à l'âme* (Paris: 1972), 88.

17. Françoise Sagan, *Le Monde*, 12 January 1985.

18. Echine, *Nouvelles littéraires*.

19. In its issue of May 1956, *La Nouvelle revue française* published a mean and retrospectively embarrassing article in which the reviewer established a list of Sagan's "favorite literary tricks."

20. Echine, *Nouvelles littéraires*.

21. "Subway, job, sleep" is the common French expression for a banal, routine, and psychologically incarcerating existence.

22. Philippe Sollers, *Le Point*, 14 May 1984.

23. Antoine Blondin, *Ma vie entre des lignes* (Paris: Table Ronde, 1982), 270.

Chapter Two

1. John G. Cawelti, *Adventure, Mystery, and Romance* (Chicago: University of Chicago Press, 1976), 1–2.

2. Rachel Blau DuPlessis, *Writing Beyond the Ending* (Bloomington: Indiana University Press, 1985), 2.

3. Sagan's three most recent novels—*Un orage immobile* (Paris, 1983), *De guerre lasse* (Paris, 1985), and *Un sang d'aquarelle* (Paris, 1987)—hold some of the fascination of the historical adventure. The former, for example, chronicles the first half of the nineteenth century while the time frame of the latter two is World War II. *Le Garde du coeur* (Paris, 1968) and *Le Chien couchant* (Paris, 1980) contain a mystery component that is as important as the love story.

4. Such aphorisms include "l'attendrissement est un sentiment agréable et entraînant comme la musique militaire" (Sentimentalism is an emotion as pleasant and compelling as military music) (*Bonjour Tristesse*, 171) and "Car enfin, tout au moins quand on est jeune, dans cette longue tricherie qu'est la vie, rien ne paraît aussi désespérément souhaitable que l'imprudence" (For, ultimately, at least when one is young, nothing seems as desperately desirable as risk in this long stream of bad jokes which constitutes life) (*Un certain sourire*, 42).

5. Although *Le Garde du coeur* was written prior to 1973, its overblown characters and parodic intent place it clearly within the major mode group.

6. Marthe Robert, *Roman des origines et origines du roman* (Paris: Grasset, 1972). This oversimplification of Robert's theory does not permit us to consider, among other useful distinctions, the one she points out between novels whose origins differ according to phases of the "family romance": (1) the "found child" fantasy (giving us fantastic/symbolic literature) and (2) the "dream of the bastard" (giving us realist works). Sagan's novels generally inscribe themselves within the second category. Robert understands the "family romance" itself as a fable that each child intuits and with which he or she lives.

7. A good example of the conventional fictional version of the family romance in saga form is the *Little House on the Prairie* series by Laura Ingalls Wilder. It is significant that these books have been adapted for television which thrives on manipulating the reigning mythology concerning masculine and feminine rapport and behavior.

8. *Bonjour Tristesse* (Paris, 1954), 21; hereafter cited in the text as *BT.*

9. A key scene in this regard occurs at the end of part 2 (chap. 4). Cécile returns from making love with Cyril for the first time and attempts to speak to Anne and light up a cigarette. As she has difficulty with both, Anne lights the cigarette for her in her own mouth and then passes it over to Cécile. By this action, she figuratively "castrates" the girl.

10. Bruno Bettelheim, *The Uses of Enchantment: The Meaning and Importance of Fairy Tales* (New York: Knopf, 1976).

11. Janice A. Radway, *Reading the Romance: Women, Patriarchy, and Popular Literature* (Chapel Hill: University of North Carolina Press, 1984).

12. Eluard's poem from his collection *La Vie immédiate* greets "sadness" with the following description: "Tu n'es pas tout à fait la misère / Car les

lèvres les plus pauvres te dénoncent / Par un sourire" (You aren't really misery, for the poorest lips denounce you with a smile).

13. *Un certain sourire* (Paris, 1956), 81; hereafter cited in the text as *UCS*.

14. Sandra Gilbert and Susan Gubar in their major study, *The Madwoman in the Attic: The Woman Writer and the Nineteenth-Century Literary Imagination* (New Haven: Yale University Press, 1979), demonstrate the prevalence in fiction of insanity and nervous disorders as metaphors for women's entrapment.

15. Sagan's three other first-person nonautobiographical novels—*Le Garde du coeur* (Paris, 1968), *Un profil perdu* (Paris, 1974), and *Un orage immobile* (Paris, 1983)—possess narrators who are, respectively, flippant, breezy, and precious. While the first two remain distanced from their stories, the third engages us in quite a different way than "Cécile" of *Bonjour Tristesse;* see chapter 5.

16. Raymond Williams, *Marxism and Literature* (Oxford: Oxford University Press, 1977).

Chapter Three

1. *Le Nouvel observateur,* 8 September 1965.

2. Interview with Bill Fuller and Robert Silvers, *Paris Review,* no. 14 (Fall 1956).

3. *Un peu de soleil dans l'eau froide* (Paris, 1969), 212; hereafter cited in the text as *PS*.

4. *Le Lit défait* (Paris, 1977), 110; hereafter cited in the text as *LD*.

5. *Aimez-vous Brahms . . .* (Paris, 1959), 119; hereafter cited in the text as *AVB*.

6. *La Chamade* (Paris, 1965), 67; hereafter cited in the text as *C*.

7. *Il fait beau jour et nuit* (Paris, 1978), 105.

8. *Paris Review,* no. 14 (Fall 1956).

9. The character Le Capitaine Elledocq of *La Femme fardée,* with his brusque manner and telegraphic language, is also a noteworthy slapstick portrait. He is, however, much less sympathetic than Florent.

10. Sagan cites Eluard's poem in the epigraph: "Inconnue, elle était ma forme préférée / Celle que m'enlèvait le souci d'être un homme / Et je la vois et je la perds et je subis / Ma douleur, comme un peu de soleil dans l'eau froide" (Unknown, she was my favorite form / The one who spared me the cares of being a man / And I see her and I lose her and I submit to / My pain, like a little sunshine in cold water).

11. Echine, *Nouvelles littéraires.*

12. Bernard Gros, *La Réforme,* 9–11 April 1969.

13. Bernard Frank, *Femme,* May 1985.

14. Rachel Brownstein, *Becoming a Heroine: Reading About Women in Novels* (New York: Viking, 1982).

15. Ibid., 296.

16. "Ciel et Terre" from "Cinq chansons inédites de Françoise Sagan," *Lettres Francaises,* no. 660 (28 February–6 March 1967). The lyrics to the entire second stanza are as follows: "Ciel et terre / dévastée / par l'ennui / l'ennui des beaux soirs d'été . . . / Solitude, de tes promesses / Il ne m'est resté que des fumées / Fumées des nuits blanches / mon coeur s'y épanche / En longs regrets . . . / Moi j'espérais qu'un jour je te quitterais / Pour quelqu'un que j'aimerais / Quelqu'un qui me garderait."

17. Colette (1873–1954), after having been relegated by numerous critics (mostly men) to the ranks of "sentimental, if clever, lady novelists," has been reassessed, thanks in great part to the women's movement, as one of the finest and most subversive writers of the first half of the twentieth century. Her deceptively simple novel *Chéri* (1920) treats the painful but dignified rupture of a six-year liaison between Léa de Lonval, a magnificent courtesan, some fifty years old, and her twenty-six-year-old paramour, whom she has always called "Chéri." Having nursed him back to health after a debauched adolescence, she then graciously prepares him to enter respectable adulthood through marriage with a proper young lady. It is Chéri who suffers a momentary breakdown after he has left the nest. Léa summons her remarkable resources to forge a new life for herself, despite holding out hope that Chéri will in fact come back to her. When he does, he sees for the first time that she is old. And she sees that he sees. As he leaves again—for good this time—she acknowledges having aged and prepares to indulge her sensuality and her joy in living in the many pleasures still left to her. Léa wins the most important battle—with herself.

Chapter Four

1. *Nouvelles littéraires,* 22 May 1969.

2. Jacqueline Piatier, *Le Monde,* 16 June 1972.

3. The Gymnase Theater, for example, which so encouraged the growth of the well-made play, still produces at least three plays a year, including in the past three of Sagan's works: *Les Violons parfois* (1961), *Le Cheval évanoui* (1966), and *L'Echarde* (1966).

4. Eric Bentley, "The Psychology of Farce," *Let's Get a Divorce! and Other Plays* (New York: Hill & Wang, 1958).

5. *Le Lit défait* (Paris, 1977), 69.

6. Poirot-Delpech, *Bonjour Sagan* (Paris: Herscher, 1984), 17.

7. Henry Rabine, *La Croix,* 23 September 1966.

8. Illuminating conversations with playwright Judith Gershman (Paris, 1985) and materials from theater programs and press clippings in the theater files of the Bibliothèque de l'Arsenal inform the discussion in this section. The popular press's treatment of Sagan's productions can be found in the Arsenal's Files.

9. *Bonheur, impair et passe, Le Cheval évanoui,* and *La Robe mauve de Val-*

entine have all been televised. While the swashbuckling *Bonheur, impair et passe* did very well reworked for television, one television viewer commented in a personal letter that *La Robe mauve de Valentine* was only interesting for the Chanel fashions that graced the production (M.-J. Bussenius, 14 May 1985). To be really thorough in the handling of Sagan as a popular dramatist—if "popular drama" is defined to also mean television and movies—one would have to discuss at length her several television pieces, including the televised versions of her plays, and her films. This material, however, is of difficult access. Moreover, Sagan has only coscripted two full-length screenplays, for *Landru* (1963) and *La Chamade* (1969), the latter one of seven films adapted by other scenarists from her novels and short stories. For the most part, reviews of the films have been quite bad, her own screenplays faring better. Again, the making of all these films has been accompanied by gossipy, somewhat hagiographic press reports, particularly because of the publicity value of their stars, for instance, Ingrid Bergman, Yves Montand, and Tony Perkins in the film *Goodbye Again* (1961) (from *Aimez-vous Brahms . . .*).

10. Elsa Triolet, *Lettres françaises*, 22 September 1966.

11. *Les Violons parfois* (Paris, 1962), 21–2.

12. Pierre Macabru, *Paris-Presse*, 14 September 1966.

13. *Un piano dans l'herbe* (Paris, 1970), 28; hereafter cited in the text as *PDH*.

14. *Bonheur, impair et passe* (Paris, 1964), 140.

15. *La Robe mauve de Valentine* (Paris, 1963), 152–53.

16. *Château en Suède* (Paris, 1960), 27–28.

17. *Le Cheval évanoui* (Paris, 1966), 82; hereafter cited in the text as *CE*.

18. *Le Figaro*, 16 July 1975.

19. Raymond Williams, *Drama from Ibsen to Brecht* (London: Penguin, 1964).

20. Ien Ang, *Watching Dallas: Soap Operas and the Melodramatic Imagination*, trans. Della Couling (London: Methuen, 1985).

Chapter Five

1. This novel caused quite a stir after its publication when the short-story writer Jean Hougron accused Sagan of plagiarizing one of his pieces. The Tribunal de Paris stopped the distribution of *Le Chien couchant* on 8 April 1981. On 7 July of the same year, Sagan and her publisher Flammarion won their own law suit against Hougron, thus acquitting her of unlawful intentions.

2. The satirical newspaper, *Le Canard enchaîné*, characterizes this brief novel as perfect reading material for one long subway ride across Paris (19 June 1968). R.-M. Albérès adds that it is "gentillement loufoque" (pleasantly wacky) (*Nouvelles littéraires*, 20 June 1968).

3. *Un sang d'aquarelle* (1987), while not as fantastical as the volumes

just mentioned, again marks a turning away from romance. Like *De guerre lasse,* this novel is set in occupied France and also traces the evolution of a main character—here Constantin Von Merk—from a carefree, bon-vivant into a death-defying participant in the French Resistance. Rather than a love affair, Von Merk's coming to terms with his former blindness to the Occupation's horrors, along with the sundry underground adventures of his intimates, provide the crux of this novel.

4. Even in her 1985 *La Maison de Raquel Véga* (The brothel of Raquel Véga), a short piece commissioned by Les Editions de la Différence, Sagan sets up a fantasy of revolt. Inspired by a painting by Colombian artist Fernando Botéro, Sagan invents a story in which the adolescent narrator-hero runs away from his privileged environment to learn about life with Mme Véga's girls.

5. Italo Calvino's insights into the fantastic—not Todorov's "physiological response to a state of uncertainty"—but, rather, "an acceptance of a different logic based on objects and connections other than those dominant in everyday life or literary conventions" is pertinent here ("Definitions of Territories: Fantasy," in *The Uses of Literature,* trans. Patrick Creagh [New York: Harcourt Brace Jovanovich, 1986], 71–72).

6. Interview with J.-L. de Rambures, *Le Monde,* 6 February 1972.

7. *Musiques de scènes* (Paris, 1981), 22; hereafter cited in the text as *MS.*

8. Tania Modleski, *Loving With a Vengeance: Mass Produced Fantasies for Women* (New York: Methuen, 1983), 13.

9. In this respect, we might consider applicable to Sagan Italo Calvino's perception of the role of sex scenes in popular culture. Calvino asserts that sexiness in popular culture compensates for the fact that sex itself is in grave danger in the contemporary big city struggle for life ("Definitions of Territory: Eroticism," 68).

10. *Un orage immobile* (Paris: 1983), 15; hereafter cited in the text as *OI.*

11. The difficulty of presenting a plot summary is compounded by Sagan's techniques of embedding one story in another and also of layering the different stories, so that, for example, the story of Nicolas's writing surfaces in both the story of his love for Flora and that of Gildas's love for Flora. The following list encompasses the several stories told by Nicolas-narrator: Nicolas comes to writing, Nicolas chronicles provincial mores, Nicolas falls in love with Flora, Gildas and Flora fall in love, Marthe explodes onto the provincial arena.

12. Bertrand Poirot-Delpech, *Le Monde,* 4 March 1983.

13. This changing focus is also true of her 1987 work, *Un sang d'aquarelle.* It commences as a social comedy but eventually turns into an adventure novel that proves a vehicle for a message of political commitment.

14. Nancy Miller, "Emphasis Added: Plots and Plausibilities in Women's Fiction," in *The New Feminist Criticism: Essays on Women, Literature, and Theory,* ed. Elaine Showalter (New York: Pantheon, 1985), 347.

15. Here, for example, is Nicolas's meditation on love in which he complains acrimoniously about the "love is war" concept operant in Sagan's third-person romances: "We're always prepared for a fight, a confrontation, but never for a union, not even for the friendship or the confidence which sometimes follows or even substitutes for passion" (*OI*, 82).

16. John Lahr, *Coward, the Playwright* (London: Methuen, 1982), 5.

17. Calvino, "Levels of Reality in Literature," 111.

18. In Proust's *Remembrance of Things Past*, the Sagan family, along with the Guermantes, represents the cream of the aristocracy. They appear intermittently throughout the many volumes of the novel, including even in its final pages.

Chapter Six

1. For the purposes of this comparison, we will rely primarily on seven of these five author's better-known texts. All but two, Cardinal's *Ecoutez la mer* and Dormann's *Je t'apporterai des orages*, have been translated into English. The novels basic to our examination include Marie Cardinal's *Ecoutez la mer* (Paris, 1962) and *Les Mots pour le dire* (Paris, 1975), Régine Deforges's *La Bicyclette bleue I* (Paris, 1981), *La Bicyclette bleue II: 10, Avenue Henri-Martin* (Paris, 1983), and *La Bicyclette bleue III: Le Diable en rit encore* (Paris, 1985), Geneviève Dormann's *Je t'apporterai des orages* (Paris, 1971), Christiane Rochefort's *Le Repos du guerrier* (Paris, 1958) and *Les Petits enfants du siècle* (Paris, 1961), and Françoise Mallet-Joris's *Le Rempart des béguines* (Paris, 1951). It goes without saying that this discussion presents merely an overview. Within the individual canons of every one of these authors (some dozen volumes of prose fiction each), exceptions to our analysis can be found. Both Christiane Rochefort's and Marie Cardinal's latest works, for example, bear witness to a more clearly proclaimed feminist bias.

2. Major contemporary women writers such as Marguerite Duras, Nathalie Sarraute, or Marguerite Yourcenar are not pertinent to this particular comparison because their experimental prose, thematic concerns, or literary obsessions disallow our including them among popular writers. (Nevertheless, as only French cultural phenomena would have it, Duras has been catapulted into the ranks of the popular since the publication of *L'Amant* in 1984.) We likewise omit such writers as Hélène Cixous, Monique Wittig, and Annie Leclerc whose work, in the case of the first two, consciously employs innovation and hermeticism in an attempt to develop a feminist aesthetics or whose texts, in the latter case, popularize the concept of "l'écriture féminine."

3. Joanna Russ, "What Can a Heroine Do? Or Why Women Can't Write," in *Images of Women in Fiction: Feminist Perspectives*, ed. Susan Koppleman Cornillon (Bowling Green: Bowling Green University Popular Press, 1972), 3–21.

4. Their daringness in sexual matters can be illustrated by citing the

1958 censorship law that led French censors to ban books by Henry Miller and William Burroughs. The moral climate up until May 1968 evidenced a great fear of sexual openness; see Herbert Lottman, *New York Times Magazine,* 28 November 1965.

    5. John Weightman, "Flirting with the Flames," *Times Literary Supplement,* 18 May 1984.

Selected Bibliography

PRIMARY SOURCES

1. Novels
Aimez-vous Brahms . . . . Paris: Julliard, 1959.
Bonjour Tristesse. Paris: Julliard, 1954.
Un certain sourire. Paris: Julliard, 1956.
La Chamade. Paris: Julliard, 1965.
Le Chien couchant. Paris: Flammarion, 1980.
Dans un mois, dans un an. Paris: Julliard, 1957.
La Femme fardée. Paris: Ramsay, 1981.
Le Garde du coeur. Paris: Julliard, 1968.
De guerre lasse. Paris: Gallimard, 1985.
Le Lit défait. Paris: Flammarion, 1977.
Les Merveilleux nuages. Paris: Julliard, 1961.
Un orage immobile. Paris: J.-J. Pauvert, 1983.
Un peu de soleil dans l'eau froide. Paris: Flammarion, 1969.
Un profil perdu. Paris: Flammarion, 1974.
Un sang d'aquarelle. Paris: Gallimard, 1987.

2. Plays
Bonheur, impair et passe. Paris: Julliard, 1964.
Château en Suède. Paris: Julliard, 1960.
Le Cheval évanoui suivi de l'Echarde. Paris: Julliard, 1966.
Il fait beau jour et nuit. Paris: Flammarion, 1979.
Un piano dans l'herbe. Paris: Flammarion, 1970.
La Robe mauve de Valentine. Paris: Julliard, 1963.
Les Violons parfois. Paris: Julliard, 1962.

3. Short Stories
Musiques de scènes. Paris: Flammarion, 1975.
Des yeux de soie. Paris: Flammarion, 1981.

4. Autobiographical Texts
Avec mon meilleur souvenir. Paris: Gallimard, 1984.
Des bleus à l'âme. Paris: Flammarion, 1972.
Réponses 1954–1974. Paris: J.-J. Pauvert, 1974.
Toxique. Drawings by Bernard Buffet. Paris: Julliard, 1964.

5. Various Short Texts

Brigitte Bardot. Commentary by Françoise Sagan; photographs by Ghislain Dussart. Paris: Flammarion, 1975.

Il est des parfums. Paris: Jean Dullis, 1973. With Guillaume Hanoteau.

Landru. Paris: Julliard, 1963. With Claude Chabrol.

La Maison de Raquel Véga. Paris: Editions de la différence, 1985.

Mirror of Venus. Photographs by Wingate Paine. N.Y.: Random House, 1966. With Frederico Fellini.

Sand et Musset: Lettres d'amour. Preface by Françoise Sagan. Paris: Herman, 1985.

Le Sang doré des Borgia. Paris: Flammarion, 1978. With Jacques Quoirez; from

6. Biography

Sarah Bernhardt: Le Rire incassable. Paris: Robert Laffont, 1987.

7. English Translations

Aimez-vous Brahms? Translated by Peter Wiles. New York: E. P. Dutton, 1960.

Bonjour Tristesse. Translated by Irene Ash. New York: E. P. Dutton, 1955.

A Certain Smile. Translated by Anne Green. New York: E. P. Dutton, 1956.

La Chamade. Translated by Robert Westhoff. New York: E. P. Dutton, 1966.

A Few Hours of Sunlight. Translated by Terence Kilmartin. New York: Harper & Row, 1971.

The Heart-keeper. Translated by Robert Westhoff. New York: E. P. Dutton, 1968.

Incidental Music. Translated by C. J. Richards. New York: E. P. Dutton, 1983.

Lost Profile. Translated by Joanna Kilmartin. New York: Delacorte Press, 1976.

Nightbird: Conversations with Françoise Sagan. Translated by David Macey. New York: Clarkson Potter, 1980.

The Painted Lady. Translated by Lee Fahnestock. New York: E. P. Dutton, 1983.

A Reluctant Hero. Translated by Christine Donougher. New York: E. P. Dutton, 1987.

Salad Days. Translated by C. J. Richards. New York: E. P. Dutton, 1984.

Scars on the Soul. Translated by Joanna Kilmartin. New York: McGraw-Hill, 1974.

Silken Eyes and Other Stories. Translated by Joanna Kilmartin. New York: Penguin, 1979.

The Still Storm. Translated by Christine Donougher. New York: E. P. Dutton, 1986.

Those Without Shadows. Translated by Frances Frenaye. New York: E. P. Dutton, 1957.

Toxique. Translated by Frances Frenaye. Illustrations by B. Buffet. New York: E. P. Dutton, 1964.

The Unmade Bed. Translated by Abigail Israel. New York: Delacorte Press/
Eleanor Friede, 1978.

With Fondest Regards. Translated by Christine Donougher. New York: E. P.
Dutton, 1985.

The Wonderful Clouds. Translated by Anne Green. New York: E. P. Dutton,
1962.

SECONDARY SOURCES

1. Bibliography

Kaiser, John Robert. "Françoise Sagan." *Bulletin of Bibliography and Magazine Notes* 30, no. 3 (July–September 1973); 106–9. Very complete bibliography until 1972 of all editions of her works, also short stories,
articles appearing in magazines including her cinema criticism, albums
with her lyrics, and translations of her works.

2. Collection

Pennsylvania State University Library. Rare Books and Special Collections.
John Robert Kaiser Collection of Françoise Sagan. First and limited editions, several original MS, theater programs, over 200 photographs, some
books and articles on Sagan—to 1972.

3. Books

Gohier-Marvier, Gérard. *Bonjour Françoise!* Paris: Editions du Grand Da-
mier, 1957. Effusive and apologetic biography of Sagan the author—the
sweet child let loose on the world, includes comments by her high school
classmates and other friends of her youth.

Hourdin, Georges. *Le Cas Françoise Sagan.* Paris: Editions du Cerf, 1958. A
fervent Catholic's reading of *Bonjour Tristesse* as an indictment of a bankrupt life-style.

Lignière, Jean. *Françoise Sagan et le succès.* Paris: Ed. du Scorpion, 1957. An
assessment of the complex attachment between Cécile and Anne in *Bonjour Tristesse* but also a veiled accusation concerning the text's authorship.

Mourgue, Gérard. *Françoise Sagan.* Paris: Editions Universitaires, 1958. A
critique from the existentialist perpective of Sagan's first three novels.

Poirot-Delpech, Bertrand. *Bonjour Sagan.* Paris: Herscher, 1985. Very
good general presentation of Sagan and especially of the cultural context in which she began her career, includes copious illustrations and
photographs.

Vandromme, Pol. *Françoise Sagan ou l'élégance de survivre.* Paris: S.E.C.L.E.–
Régine Deforges, 1977. Excessively lyrical and impressionistic overview
of Sagan's style and her life.

4. Articles

Brophy, Brigid. "Françoise Sagan and the Art of the Beau Geste." *Texas Quarterly* 7, no. 4 (Winter 1964):59–69. Sympathetic and perceptive overview of Sagan's work until 1964.

Cismaru, Alfred. "Françoise Sagan's Theory of Complicity." *Dalhousie Review*, Winter 1965–66, 457–69. Deft plot summaries of works through *Bonheur, impair et passe* and attempt to understand all of them according to the common theme of freedom's limits and imperatives.

Echine, Jean-Louis. "Entretien: Sagan sans clichés." *Nouvelles littéraires*, 7 April 1977, 5. One of the best interviews with Sagan published after those collected in 1974 in *Réponses (Nightbird)*.

Engel, Marian. *"Scars on the Soul."* *New York Times Book Review*, 14 April 1974, 6–7. Very good assessment of Sagan's style in general and of *Scars on the Soul* in particular.

Fuller, Blair, and Silvers, Robert. "The Art of Fiction XV: Françoise Sagan." *Paris Review*, Autumn 1956, 83–91. Excellent early interview with Sagan about coming to writing.

Garis, Leslie. "Sagan: Encore Tristesse." *New York Times Magazine*, 16 November 1980, 64–72, 88–104. Entertaining retrospective of Sagan's work and life with a focus on her published interviews in *Nightbird*.

Josselin, Jean-François. "Les Années Sagan." *Nouvel observateur*, 18 March 1983, 14–17. Excellent interview with Sagan, who discusses her own work, particularly *Un orage immobile*.

"Precocious Parisienne." *Life Magazine*, 16 May 1955, 97–102. Famous photographic documentary on Sagan on the occasion of her first visit to the U.S.

Updike, John. "Books." *New Yorker*, no. 25 (12 August 1974):95–99. Good critique of *Scars on the Soul* and an overview of Sagan, who, as a popular novelist, "keeps us company."

Index